Training the Retriever

TRAINING THE RETRIEVER

A manual

J. A. Kersley

Sketches by James Croft
Photographs by Arthur Robinson

POPULAR DOGS
London Melbourne Sydney Auckland Johannesburg

Popular Dogs Publishing Co. Ltd
An imprint of the Hutchinson Publishing Group
3 Fitzroy Square, London W1P 6JD

Hutchinson Group (Australia) Pty Ltd
30–32 Cremorne Street, Richmond South, Victoria 3121
PO Box 151, Broadway, New South Wales 2007

Hutchinson Group (NZ) Ltd
32–34 View Road, PO Box 40-086, Glenfield, Auckland 10

Hutchinson Group (SA) (Pty) Ltd
PO Box 337, Bergvlei 2012, South Africa

First published 1970
Second edition, revised 1973
Third edition 1976
Fourth edition 1978
Fifth edition 1980

© J. A. Kersley 1970, 1973, 1976, 1978 and 1980

James Croft's sketches
© Popular Dogs Publishing Co. Ltd 1970

Appendix 2 © The Kennel Club 1977

Appendix 3 © The Kennel Club 1977

Printed in Great Britain at The Anchor Press Ltd
and bound by Wm Brendon & Son Ltd
both of Tiptree, Essex

ISBN 0 09 134510 3

To Kenneth Atkinson
'the gentle handler'
who trained the author

Contents

	Author's preface	8
	Foreword by F. Kenneth Atkinson	9
1	Introduction	11
2	Know your dog	17
3	On scent and scenting	27
4	On choosing a puppy: its housing and management	35
5	The first year	46
6	The training ground—the rabbit pen	51
7	On crime and punishment and the correction of faults	57
8	Handling	65
9	Training	75
10	Obstacles and how you hope to surmount them	94
11	Advanced handling	105

12	Advanced training	115
13	The errors of an amateur	121
14	The first and second seasons	127
15	On judges and judging	135
16	Of guns, stewards and professional trainers	142
17	Working tests and field trials	145
18	The final bounce	155
	Appendices	
1	*Retriever Societies*	160
2	*Guide to Field Trial Judges (Retrievers)*	164
3	*Kennel Club Field Trial Rules (Extracts)*	168
	Index	185

Author's Preface to the Second Edition

On occasions when I have been asked to describe retriever training simply and in a few words, I have answered as follows:

'The longer I train retrievers the more I consider that the first twelve months, even the first six, of a puppy's life are of prime importance. Like a human baby he is establishing habit patterns quite unconsciously. These patterns will last him all his life and if the wrong ones are established they are difficult to eradicate. Teaching him baby hunting, retrieving, giving him love and elementary ideas of obedience are essential during this period to integrate him into his surroundings in a strange world. After all, this training occurs in Nature and the reason why we tend to neglect it is because the results are not obvious.

'During the second period of training, which may last from six months to a year—time being of no importance and some dogs taking a long time to develop —of the many lessons he has to learn, respect for his master is the most important. Insistence on obedience to every order and severe enough punishments meted out to command this respect and obedience is essential. It is during this period that if you wear out your new car on your dog you will have a good dog. New cars are plentiful; good dogs are not!

'Finally there comes a definite day, which I often ring in red on my calendar, when suddenly patience and perseverance are rewarded and the dog appears to know it all; from an awkward, perverse youngster, he has become overnight a mature dog.

'Then follows a polishing period which is the most interesting and rewarding time in training, and this will go on throughout the dog's active life. However, if this is neglected, all the previous training is wasted effort.'

On being asked to write a preface to the second edition of this book, I had to consider what changes I would like to have made in it. Firstly, should I have emphasised discipline more, as discipline is essential? I asked Jack Chudley this question. He paused, then looked at me and said, 'If I have to thump a dog to train it, I get rid of the dog'. At the moment I have, in fact, under training, one of Jack's dogs which is one of the most intelligent and obedient I have had.

Perhaps I made the book rather short, but if I had made it longer it might have missed its point—that is to say, clear-cut guide lines for amateurs to enable them to reach a high standard of training. It has been known to happen that when I have become slack in my training methods, or in handling, I have referred to my own book to see where I have gone wrong!

Since this book was published in 1970, I have not changed my training methods in any way.

I would like to thank the 6,000-odd readers, both British and American, who have made this second edition of *Training the Retriever* necessary, and especially those of them who have written to me saying that the book has helped them in their own training. I would also like to thank Mr. Gerald Austin of Hutchinson, who has so patiently and diligently guided an enthusiastic amateur writer in the paths of professionalism.

Finally, I would like my readers to remember that you can't make a pig into a racehorse but that, if you try hard enough, you can own a very fast pig.

1973   J.A.K.

Author's Preface to the Third, Fourth and Fifth Editions

It has given me great pleasure to realize that this book has required third, fourth and fifth editions so soon after the second. The appendices have, therefore, been three times brought up to date, but otherwise there have been few changes to the text, and I can only hope that my new readers will enjoy the book as much as my previous readers seem to have done.

1976, 1978, 1980   J.A.K.

F. Kenneth Atkinson

Foreword

For many years I have shot with Jack Kersley, who has always been interested in good dog work.

Some years ago his old dog died and he purchased a puppy of good working strain. He came along to my place, and we have trained together ever since. All the lessons he described in his book have been used many times and proved most satisfactory. Lately he has had considerable success at Field Trials. Many a shooting man makes the excuse when his dog misbehaves that he hasn't the time to train his dog properly. In fact this is not so, as a short period of leisure time devoted to training will be very rewarding—and much more pleasure will be had on shooting days.

This book can be divided into three parts. The first is on knowing how and why an animal behaves. After all, unless you know your dog it is impossible to achieve any success.

The second part deals with day-to-day training from

puppyhood. It is my belief that someone who has not trained a dog before could, by following these methods, train one to a high standard. Most guns will admit that the standard of dog work at many shoots is very low.

The third part deals with advanced training, field trials and so on. I particularly like the chapter on scent which throws another light on this very complex problem. Jack Kersley began writing some time ago when he was on holiday abroad and has added his experiences from time to time, proving the system of training by practical experience. There is no reason why any sportsman, after following his methods, so simply described and easy to follow, should not have a steady and reliable retriever.

'Some dogs are very great, like the Wolf Dog which is shaped like a Greyhound but much taller, longer and thicker; some are for the Buck, others for the Boar, Bear and Bull; some for the Hare, Coney and Hedgehog; some are both for water and land, and they are called Spaniels; others are called Lurchers, Tumblers, Brachers and Beagles, etc. As for shepherd dogs, foisting curs, and such whom some fond lady make their daily, nay nightly companions too, I shall pass over, being neither worthy to be inserted in this subject nor agreeable thereunto: Wherefore I shall only treat of such whose nature do incline them to game for man's pastime and recreation.'

The Gentleman's Recreation
Nicholas Cox, 1674

*'Hark, hark, the dogs do bark,
The beggars are coming to town'*

1 An introduction

The amateur who undertakes the training of a dog must be an enthusiast. After he has chosen with considerable care a suitable puppy, he begins training and in the next eighteen months allots a small period of each day to the animal, only to find towards the end of this time that the dog is hard-mouthed, impossibly headstrong, is a 'yipper', or has an unfortunate and uncontrollable temperament under stress; indeed the dog may not have the basic mental and physical qualities necessary to achieve even moderate success in the field. The amateur must then start again from the beginning. This has been summed up with considerable truth in the following saying:
  'Neither Jack Chudley, Dick Male, Uncle Tom Cobley,
    nor the Beverley Sisters can train temperament!'
It is not always easy to spot the faults in a dog at an early date. Your brilliant and docile youngster of his first season often becomes, when he is adolescent and more mature, the hard, headstrong dog of the second season. On the other hand, many a difficult youngster that nobody wants has been trained into

a brilliant dog by infinite patience and understanding. The amateur must therefore be prepared to cull as early as possible. The professional, however, who rears many dogs and has a large kennel, culls his dogs without mercy until he has one which he thinks is a winner. There is a certain amount of good-natured rivalry between professional and amateur, and certainly the amateur is very proud if he can run his dog against the professionals at trials and get away with it. The professional maintains that the amateur can spend endless time and trouble on one dog; the amateur on the other hand envies the professional his opportunities of running several dogs and of choosing the best on which to concentrate for trials. He also envies the professional his wide experience of handling and knowledge of dogs which can only be obtained by years of experience. Given the right dog, however, there is no reason why the amateur should not at least hold his own with the professional handler, and if he does so due credit is given him.

A dog is essentially a pack animal. In prehistoric times dogs no doubt tended to scrounge round the caves of human beings. This prehistoric man may have welcomed and encouraged, as the dog would give warning of the approach of danger. Probably a child found a puppy one day and her father allowed her to keep it rather than knock it on the head and put it in the pot. Unfortunately, even today puppies are reared and fattened for food in the Far East!

Thus it came about that domestic dogs evolved, and throughout the ages gaunt hound dogs, four or five at a time, have been used to track down rebels and criminals, their master riding on horseback with them. Hounds were used also for hunting game, often for driving them into nets or, in the case of the fox, to ground, and they were also used to drive game so that the hunters could shoot it with their bows, or later guns. Hares were hunted by a dog similar to the present-day greyhound, the hare being in those days very much more prized for food than was the rabbit. Gradually the use of dogs has become more specialised until they have reached the very high standard achieved today.

In the olden days training was at times very cruel to the quarry—for instance the instructions Cox gives for training hounds to a fox or hart were as follows:

> Take an old Fox, or Badger, and cut away the nether Jaw, but meddle not with the other, leaving the upper to shew the fury of the Beast, although it can do no harm therewith. Here note, that instead of cutting away the Jaw it will be every whit as well to break out all his Teeth, to prevent him from biting the Terriers.

Or,

> There are several ways of entering Hounds. As first, by taking a Hart in nets, and after you have cut off one of his Feet, let him go: a quarter hour after, assemble your young Hounds, and having found out the View or Slot of the Hart or Buck by your Bloodhounds, uncouple your young Hounds, and let them hunt.

We have, however, advanced since those days and, in spite of the accusations of the League against Cruel Sports, we try to the best of our ability to be cruel neither to our dogs nor to the game we hunt.

Dogs to this day have preserved their instincts for living and working in a pack, but have adopted human beings as pack members. In the home the dog acknowledges his master as pack leader and the other members of the household in varying degree. For instance, to his master's wife and other residents in the home he may well be civil and accept them, but he considers them lower in the pack or peck order. It must never be expected of a dog that he treat a human being otherwise than he would another member of the pack or his pack leader. Other dogs he challenges until he has fitted them into their correct status, usually winning by seizing the other dog by the neck and shaking him. This form of punishment—of seizing a dog by the neck and shaking him—we use in training.

Each dog has individual characteristics, but broadly they

are divided into three main types. The 'Peter Pan' dog never grows up—an amiable idiot, he is childishly dependent on anybody and everybody but owes individual allegiance to none, loving everybody indiscriminately. He will not make a brilliant gun dog as he is incapable of mature and intelligent action. Secondly, there is the mature and independent dog who for a very different reason owes allegiance to none. He is capable of biting and attacking a man in the same way as he would another dog, and from time to time he will challenge his master's leadership. He will accept a beating but it will have no effect on him, as he will wag his tail and almost immediately and quite happily commit the same fault again—in the natural world he would become the pack leader. Many highly intelligent but really dominant dogs are virtually untrainable because they refuse any leadership except their own. Thirdly and in between there is the ideal dog who, while accepting discipline and being friendly and polite to strangers, has complete loyalty to his master and is adult enough to act independently.

The object of training is to encourage the animal's natural abilities, at the same time having the dog in complete control in all situations and at all times. At the end of the last century dog owners allowed their dogs to run completely free and then placed them under hard discipline to get control. This succeeded up to a point, but it must be remembered that the dogs were not so finely bred and probably many more dogs were discarded than even today. Nor was the standard of training so high.

The humanitarians stepped in and the pendulum swung the other way. The dog was completely trained from a puppy and obeyed the slightest signal from his master. He could be put on a sixpence at one hundred yards. Thus a type of circus dog was produced who would only hunt to order. Now the pendulum has swung more central and, while the dog is infinitely more obedient, he still hunts with style, is free-running and uses his intelligence.

The Americans, however, still desire more of a circus dog than we do. I am told that they often buy a good dog from

Britain at two and a half to three years of age and retrain it. Their field trials are more like working tests in which live game are released and shot in various situations for the dogs to find. However satisfying it may be to the vanity of the owner to be able to put his dog exactly where he wants it, it is a far more beautiful sight to see an intelligent dog working stylishly and looking to his handler only when he thinks he is at fault.

Dogs are trained for an astonishing variety of activities, but all training is basically the same—to encourage a dog's natural abilities and intelligence on the one hand, and to instil obedience to his master on the other. These aims are somewhat opposed: as the natural ability of the animal is encouraged, obedience is reduced and when obedience is insisted upon, speed and free running are necessarily restricted. A dog, for example, employed on hound trails needs little obedience, while a dog trained simply to take part in obedience tests need not use any intelligence. As I have pointed out, in the field trial dog of today we try to achieve a perfect balance between these two aims, and by our achievement of this balance our success is judged.

This book is on the training of the 'non-slip retriever'. These pure retrievers consist of black, yellow and chocolate labradors, golden retrievers, chesapeakes, flat and curly-coated retrievers, and poodles! It is emphasised that all varieties of retrievers are trained in exactly the same manner.

The ideal retriever is considered to be one whose reflexes have been so conditioned that he obeys every signal of his master immediately and without thinking, but goes out freely with speed and style, and has basic confidence not only in his master but in himself; a dog who, if he finds himself at fault, immediately looks to his master for help but when told to hunt methodically covers his ground and returns again and again to the fall if he does not find; a dog, therefore, who has perseverance and does not lose his head; a dog who has the courage to face difficult cover, who jumps without fear, faces fast-running water when asked to do so and is always capable of working on his own if his master is out of sight. This is a classic dog and if it were easy to obtain him, there would be no fun in training or trials.

I have always found in textbooks that it is impossible to find the answer to your particular problem. It is also not possible to learn an art through a book of instruction. The skill in an art is only acquired by practice, and the craftsman learns as he goes along. I am hoping, however, that this book is sufficiently practical and detailed to set the novice off on the right course. If he is serious in his endeavours he will find many friends, both amateur and professional, who will help him by correcting his faults and encouraging his success.

This is a book written by an amateur for amateurs, although I hope my professional friends may get a little quiet amusement out of it. It is written while the difficulties of training are fresh in my mind—the professional has often forgotten the difficulties that troubled him in the early days. It sometimes wanders from the strict path of training—but after all this is how training should go—and I have tried to introduce a little humour. Whether I have written about a serious subject in a light manner or a light subject in a serious manner, I leave to the reader to decide according to his temperament. Any humour found in this book, whether contrived or accidental is, however, purely coincidental!

*'Is thy servant a dog
that thou comest at me with staves?'*

2 Know your dog

To train a dog successfully, it is not only necessary to understand the physical and mental capabilities of dogs in general but also to understand the particular dog you have under training.

A dog's eyesight approximates to that of a keen-sighted old man—he is long-sighted but does not focus near objects. A dog can mark the fall of a bird with extreme accuracy at a hundred yards or so. He can focus on an object and have a clearly defined image of the object over hundreds of yards. Near to, however, his eyesight is less reliable and he tends not to use it, exactly like the old man. A dog is colourblind and sees everything in monochrome. His retina does not contain the cells necessary to distinguish colour. Close objects therefore have less contrast and are more difficult to distinguish.

All animals, including man, have two types of vision—central and peripheral. The central area of the retina of the eye shows the shape and size of an object, while the peripheral area only appreciates movement and shadowy forms, and then instructs the animal to turn his eyes towards the moving object to visualise it more closely. The relative importance and sensitivity of these two types of vision varies, however, between animals and man, central vision being less acute in animals and peripheral vision more acute. A dog seldom looks directly at another dog who is near him for any prolonged period of time as this constitutes a challenge, but instead the two present their backsides to each other. The peripheral vision of a dog, on the other hand, is more sensitive than that of a man because it is a safety factor to enable him either to fight or flee from his enemy. If a man stares at an animal, it will put him out of countenance and you can punish a dog by holding his head and staring at him—so behave as an animal behaves, be polite and do not rudely stare, especially at strangers. The proper approach to an animal is to be aware of him but to ignore him and let him make the advances—exactly the same way as one would behave to a child.

A dog's vision takes over where his nose ceases to function. While human beings have visual brains, a dog has a nasal brain. It is estimated that a dog can distinguish thirty thousand different smells! How this was worked out I have no idea. However, I would not dispute it. After all, we can differentiate thousands of different objects. A human being will linger over a delightful view; a dog will linger over an interesting smell, however repulsive this may be to our nostrils. We live in a beautiful world of colours and a dog lives in a beautiful world of scents.

A dog can, with the wind favourable, smell a dummy hidden in a tussock at forty to fifty yards, turn in his tracks and go and pick it unerringly. How much more easily found must be a hot, freshly-killed pheasant with the blood smell upon it! However, if a bird or a dummy is placed against a fence with the wind blowing away from the dog, he will usually not see it and not be able to smell it even within a range of a few feet.

Everything that is going on about him is recognised by his sense of smell. He also has a shrewd understanding of all that has happened in his vicinity for the last twenty-four hours.

It is interesting to contemplate what would happen if the human race had the same gift. Certainly there would be an improved morality amongst married couples. I can imagine the husband coming home and his wife saying, 'Edward, you've been with that dreadful woman, Mary, again—and you rang me up and said you'd be late at the office!' Or the husband saying, 'Elizabeth, that ghastly bounder, Fred, has been here again, and what has he been doing in our bedroom—waiting for a bus!'

A dog's hearing differs in three respects from that of a man: it is far more acute; it has a far wider range, especially to high frequencies; and it is more sensitive to vibration. There is a temptation when standing at a covert shoot to place your dog in front of you where you can see what the wretched animal is doing. This is a mistake in that he will get the full muzzle blast of your gun and be deafened.

The silent whistle is the use we make of the dog's ability to hear very high tones and it is effective at an incredible range, provided your dog has been trained to obedience at long distances.

Fish have no ears as such but along their sides is a series of sensitive areas which react to vibrations in the water. Very primitive animals, such as prehistoric lizards, had no ears as we know them but received vibrations through their skeletal structure. This is true also of snakes. Shout at an adder and he will not hear, but take one step forward and he will glide away. The earthworm also feels the patter of rain and comes to the surface, and there are no doubt many more examples in nature of hearing through vibrations.

There is no doubt that the dog can hear ground vibrations at a very long distance better than we can. A dog marks a fall, notably by vision but also by hearing the thump, and to enforce an order a stamp of the foot is an effective means of expression and probably carried up to fifty yards.

In training a dog on unseen dummies, care must be taken that the dog has not seen, has not heard, and has no foot scent to guide him to where the dummy lies.

It must be realised that a dog never moves or acts without reason—he hasn't a very big mind but it is an extremely logical one. Therefore it is your job to get into the little mind of your dog. Have you noticed that if there is no reason for him to do anything at any particular time, he usually goes to sleep He is a slow learner, not because he is incapable of learning, but owing to language difficulties there is a lack of interpretation. In a puppy it is a lack of comprehension on his part and a lack of means of expression on your part that make the difficulty in training. Unfortunately, later when the puppy grows older he develops a will and personality of his own and where as a puppy he would disobey an order which he understood because he wanted to play, later he will disobey an order through defiance or because he thinks he knows better than his master. This is exactly the same as a child and his father. In fact, any man who can bring up a child successfully can train a dog! It is regrettable that so few people can bring up children successfully. The opposite is probably not true. A dog can be put in a kennel when he becomes a nuisance and need only be taken out when both master and dog are on their best behaviour.

Every animal has a definite distance at which, when approached by a superior force or something strange and alien, he will turn and run away. This is the 'flight' distance. Likewise there is another critical distance at which, if he is surprised by an enemy, he will immediately attack—this is the 'fight' distance.

Any animal will bite if he is cornered and cannot escape. Sometimes, however, a dog may bite rather unexpectedly—for instance, a dog may go up to a stranger, lie on his back and ask to be tickled, but then bite the hand which is put down to tickle his tummy. This is not treachery but biting from fear of being touched.

Whether a dog has other senses not known to human beings is debatable. It is known that dogs can find their way home over long distances. For instance, I had a dog which I bought when it was aged about fifteen months, and transferred to its new home about fifty miles away. It escaped and I contacted the late owner. The dog had not gone back there but was recaptured a week later at the kennels where it was born, about fifty miles in the opposite direction! This is a true story and is very hard to explain.

There are many stories of dogs seeing ghosts, their hair going up and their behaviour being out of character. Is this a form of extra-sensory perception, or are we being spoofed, not spooked

It is interesting to consider how animals use their excreta. The human race is ashamed of this function of their bodies but even in civilised countries it was not always so. In the Court of Versailles before the French Revolution, there were four hundred bedrooms and no privies! It was often only considered necessary to have a screen placed round a chamber pot in the salon. In Mexico today there is still in existence a house with a bath and two lavatories in one room where presumably friends can go and sit down and have a chat!

The rhino marks out his territory by walking round the boundary and defecating at intervals. Any stranger who then enters his territory is challenged.

A dog has the happy knack of saving his urine and letting it out in small jets to let his friends and enemies know where he has been. He will also do this sometimes to food or objects he values to establish ownership. Birds have a far more aesthetic method of singing their challenges from the treetops.

A dog will eat the excreta of any herbiferous animal but not that of a carnivore, presumably because its diet is lacking in half-digested vegetable residues. However, he will roll in the faeces of any animal so as to disguise his scent when out hunting.

Before you can be expected to know much about a dog, it is necessary to work with it for a month or two. The new dog will not, in fact, accept you as its leader under this time. During this period you get to know your dog and your dog gets to understand you. Sometimes I wonder which is the more important! It is therefore essential that before you can begin training in earnest you establish a good relationship with your dog founded on respect, mutual affection and trust, and understanding.

Many dogs, however, are incapable of being trained for the shooting field. How many more are unfit for field trials owing to either mental or physical disability! Some dogs with the right temperament are keyed up but behave superbly on the big occasions. Others, although behaving beautifully under training conditions, become over-excited and unmanageable in a hot corner; finally something snaps in their brain and they forget all their training.

The special relationship that animals develop between themselves is beloved of the popular press. A pregnant elephant with an auntie to look after her who defends her during the birth of the calf and then helps her with the calf's upbringing is a case in point.

I had a whippet once who at mealtimes would always fetch a dirty little mongrel friend into the house and watch him feeding from her bowl before she would eat herself. An Alsatian of mine helped my bitch in whelp to dig a large cave under a rotten tree where she wished to have her pups. When they were born, he obviously considered himself quite erroneously to be the father!

Jealousy and malice, of course, always exist. Bitches should never be left together unless they know each other, as they may snap at each other and injure themselves with their canine teeth, proving that the female of the species is more deadly than the male! A bitch puppy should never be left with an older bitch as the puppy may be bullied and turned out in the cold on a winter's night if they are kennelled together.

A puppy is as forgetful as a child and has to have the same lesson taught him over and over again. Once he has mastered the lesson, however, he has a good memory: it becomes an integral part of his make-up and he will never forget it. This is also similar to the psychology of a child. Each child, his parents know, has to be treated differently and this also applies to dogs. A dog will remember for ever the owner who had him in puppyhood however long they have been separated. This excellent memory was appreciated by Homer. It may be remembered that Odysseus, on returning to Ithaca after his adventures, which had taken many years, was not recognised by his court or friends but was immediately welcomed by his blind old hound.

I knew an owl once with a long memory. A big game hunter, living in England, took a couple of owlets from their nest and put them in his aviary. He christened them Dopey and Churchill. When they were nine months old he gradually set them free and then returned to Kenya himself.

Unfortunately for him, he was mauled by a leopard and invalided to England. About eighteen months later he was walking through a wood when he saw an owl, so he gave his feeding whistle. The owl floated down and perched on his shoulder and accompanied him back about three miles to the country club where he was living. Churchill—for the owl obviously was Churchill—then took up residence in the club and in the evening when the windows were open he would fly into the bar and perch on some unsuspecting guest's bare shoulders; or a guest on waking would find Churchill perched on her pillow! After the first few incidents, every visitor to the club had to be warned. Churchill, when he was hungry, soon learned to walk into the kitchen and demand food. Unfortunately, a superstitious Irish cook was engaged and this man decided that the owl had brought him bad luck. One day Churchill's body was found in the kitchen dustbin with his neck wrung. This true story is a delightful cameo of life, but I seem to have strayed from dogs and we must now get back to retrievers.

The history of the Labrador is interesting and helps us to understand the qualities of the breed. Labradors arrived in this country about 1800, having been brought over from Newfoundland by the fishermen. There were two types: the Newfoundland dog, a big strong specimen with its tail curved over its back, which was used to drag the sleighs and help the fishermen with hauling in their nets; and the smaller type, the St. John's breed, which was used for retrieving fish and no doubt other forms of game. This was a profitable trade on both sides until, it is said, the Excise Officers stepped in and charged too much duty, when the trade ceased. By this time, however, the nobility and gentry had come to appreciate their characteristics so much that they crossed their Labradors with flat-coats and other sporting dogs, and even with sheepdogs.

Colonel Hawker has described the true Labrador of the period as 'very long, strong in limb, rough-haired, and carried the tail high'—a breed which we can recognise today. Another type he described as 'long in the head and nose, deep in the chest, very fine in the legs, with smooth hair and does not carry his tail curled, and is exceedingly good at running, swimming and fighting.' This smaller type—presumably the St. John's—was described as being 'smaller, more easily managed and sagacious in the extreme.'

After the Kennel Club was formed, cross-breeding was discouraged and Labradors have reverted to a true breed. Occasionally signs of the sheepdog or the flat-coat reappear, but I think that the two types of dog describes by Hawker still exist today.

The finished product

What should a Labrador look like? He is going to be a working dog so appearance is not of great importance. However, perhaps one should have some kind of standard. Obviously he should have a pleasant expression and handsome head; broad forehead, good stop, brown kindly eyes and wide nostrils. He should have a good bite and powerful jaws, which it is hoped he will not use, with even teeth—no malocclusion for us! He should have a large chest with a long, strong neck and strong back quarters; he should be close coupled. The Americans allow some slope from back to rear but this is frowned upon in Britain. He should have an 'otter tail'—wide and thick at the base, short and tapering with no feathering. He should be a tail-wagger. It is often said that a dog does not find with his tail but I have never known a judge not to be impressed by a busy dog with a wagging tail—at least it points to amiability of character.

The Labrador should have reasonable bone but be neither cow-hocked, bandy-legged, knock-kneed, spavined, spread out at elbows, or ricketty. So he should be straight-legged with reasonable angulation behind. He should have a thick undercoat and a rather rough overcoat, although a silky overcoat is very pleasing but frowned upon. A Labrador should not have curls and waves are definitely out! He should not be too big. The small dogs are the quickest, the big dogs are the strongest. The quick little dog, however, will beat a heavy slow one at any time and the small ones will go where the big ones cannot. He should have that indefiniable attribute, quality, which is partly physical fitness, partly pride in himself and self-confidence, and partly balanced beauty. He should move well. By watching between retrieves one can see if a dog is shivering or his teeth are chattering, or if he is panting—these are all signs of nerves. If he is quietly lying down chewing the grass or if he is sitting up quietly taking an intelligent interest in proceedings, he has a good temperament—a dog soon knows when he is not going to be sent out.

A show Labrador may be considered as a box, the ratio of whose length to depth is two to one, with four approximately equal and medium-sized legs at the corners, equipped with good solid feet on them, a short, wide lever at one end and a rugged buttress of a chest at the other.

I do not consider such a Labrador to be a very handsome animal, and to say he is muscle-bound is perhaps an uncharitable exaggeration. Beauty is in the eye of the beholder! Certainly he is a reasonably functional animal but not as functional as, for example, the Alsatian, which to my mind has the perfect balance of function and beauty.

The show Labrador is not equipped for speed, but then he is not supposed to chase. He is a strong dog who on occasion can take up very beautiful attitudes. I think, however, that some elegant and intelligent working Labradors who could not appear in the show ring are more functionally pleasing. We must continue to strive for the perfect animal which has brains, beauty and balance.

'Eh, it's a queer thing is scent!'

3 On scent and scenting

If you talk to a huntsman about scent, as like as not he will pause deep in thought and then say, 'Eh, but it's a queer thing is scent!'—but of course scent follows the law of physics as do other natural phenomena. First it must be kept in mind that there are two kinds of scent: (1) air scent, and (2) ground scent. A dog running on air scent will follow several yards down wind of the actual track. If he is running off ground scent his nose will be to the ground, snuffling as he goes along. Air scent depends on the vagaries of the wind. Ground scent is, of course, a fixed line.

There are also two kinds of objects emitting scent—one the actual quarry itself, the other the place where it has passed or brushed as it fell or moved, but these react somewhat differently.

Molecules of scent are absorbed by surface tension on to droplets of moisture. This gives the molecules mass but little weight. Then the droplets move away from the object, scattering in all directions. This is brought about by radiation, or by the object breathing or moving and setting up eddy currents. But before the molecules move far they are caught up in convection currents and usually start rising, as hot air rises; then puffs of wind carry the molecules with them downwind, like smoke from a steam engine. It is thus clear that the first physical effect necessary to provide good scenting conditions is the provision of moisture—a warm, steamy day as opposed to a hot and dry one. Next we want a good temperature variation between the quarry, the ground on which it has fluttered, and the air above it to provide good convection currents.

In the early morning the earth is chilled. It is not possible for vaporisation to take place and scenting may be bad. By mid-morning the earth has heated up, radiates heat waves into the air and sets up convection currents. By midday the sun is really hot and the earth and air temperatures may be similar and scent falls off, but in late afternoon the air is cooling, the hot earth is radiating again and scent once more improves.

Next there is the actual texture of the ground itself and how much cover is growing on it. Bare ground is not contaminated sufficiently to hold the scent, while a field with really thick herbage does not let the wind get to it. In between there is the ground with adequate cover, but the cover is light enough to let the wind collect the scent.

Strength of wind, of course, is also important. Too strong a wind, while it carries the scent long distances, will disperse it. A light, steady wind will assist your dog the most. Upwind radiation or eddy currents must be measured in inches rather than feet or yards, so that the dog may pass the quarry very close upwind and not smell it.

Further, the particular scent of the quarry should be given some consideration. As a policeman with tracker dogs would say, 'A ripe old tramp dripping with lice who has not seen a bath for the last ten years is more delectable to my dogs than the hygienic gentleman who takes his daily bath, has many suits of clothes and changes his linen at frequent intervals.'

Making the most of the scent

Above is a sketch to show how even in one field scenting conditions can vary from very good to very bad. Under the bank and with thick cover the scent is poor—elsewhere the scent is better.

Above A pheasant has fallen through the trees into the wood with only light undercover and is lying in full view. The dog is sent to retrieve it but, ignoring the pheasant, he tries to climb the tree from which the pheasant has fallen. Although sent back to try again, again he tries to climb the tree! In this case it is possible that, while the air is hot, the ground under the trees is cool. The pheasant has brushed the leaves of the trees and here there is a down convection current from the hot upward air towards the cold ground.

Opposite above A bird lying in full view on the edge of a runnel with the wind blowing over the runnel towards the bird will often be missed as the dog will search the more interesting ditch and fail to scent the bird in full view on the bank.

A partridge lying on its back in the middle of a bare open field is notoriously difficult to pick. The reason for this rather inexplicable difficulty is that the bird is on its back because

it was shot stone dead in the air and therefore has not fluttered. There is, therefore, little contamination of the surrounding ground and in any case the field is bare and is not holding the scent. The wind is probably playing over the partridge so that its feathers are flattened and not ruffled, keeping radiation to a minimum. For the same reason a pheasant in her nest gives very little scent. She approaches the nest quietly in a straight line, leaving little track scent. Then she settles with her head into the wind so that the breeze does not ruffle her feathers.

The olfactory areas in the brain fatigue rapidly. If the smell is removed, however, there is a short latent period and then heightened sensitivity. If the smell is continued after a short time it can no longer be smelled. But this fatigue is specific to the stimulus causing it and other scents can be appreciated normally. A dog can be put off if it has to track across an area where a herd of cows has been milling about and stirring up the mud and defecating, until some measure of fatigue to this strong smell has been established. It is this fatigue which enables a dog with bad teeth and halitosis to scent normally and humans to be unaware of their bad breath unless their best friends tell them! To what extent fatigue occurs in the shooting field it is impossible to tell as all experiments on fatigue, as far as I know, have been performed on human beings, who have far less sensitive and more ridumentary olfactory areas.

A pack of hounds runs on air scent. It has been stated that a hare, after being hunted for some time, loses its scent, and it has been known for a hard-hunted hare to squat and the pack to swoop over it and carry on for a hundred yards or so and then start questing for the quarry. I do not believe that a hard-hunted hare loses its scent—in fact it should be increased —the tired hare is running with its belly to the ground, or its legs may be stiff and are longer in contact with the ground. Its leaps are shorter and it is hotter and sweating and will be leaving more scent. However, being tired, it may squat in a hollow. The leaders of the pack, if the hare is running downwind, as it may do especially if tired, will swoop over it, not using their eyesight and running on air scent, and the rest of the pack will follow. The air scent will have carried fifty to a hundred yards downwind and the momentum of the pack will take the leaders and the pack itself another fifty yards, so the hunt will be carried well past where the hare is squatting and in due course, unless the pack is recast, the hare will creep off quietly to safety.

Some people think that there is a special smell of fear. Fear or anger leads to the liberation of adrenalin in the blood with consequent sweating if there are any sweat glands—dogs, for instance, have none—increased pulse and respiration rates with an increased blood supply to the legs, brain, lungs and voluntary muscles—a protective mechanism. This increased activity may add to the scent given off by the animal. To the victim of the angry lion the whole world must be filled with his acrid, musty smell, and the smiling cat's appetite is sharpened as the timorous, squealing mouse emits that delicious mousy odour! It is however, a blood scent that the Retriever relies upon to retrieve his quarry and, of course, your well-trained dog should never pick a quarry unless it has been wounded.

There are many stories of how animals try to confuse their scent when hunted, by taking to water, by doubling on their tracks, by leaping sideways, by running down one side of a hedge and then up the other, by running through a herd of cows or sheep, by starting up another animal of the same kind. Some of these tricks must be considered as conscious thought, others perhaps as chance. However, they belong to the hunting field and not to the shooting world. The only trick we know is when a wounded pheasant takes sanctuary in a rabbit-hole.

Let us see what our friend Nicholas Cox has to say about scent:

> In frosty weather the scent freezeth with the Earth, so that there is no certainty of hunting till it thaw, or that the Sun arise. Likewise if very much Rain fall between the starting of the Hare and time of hunting, it is not convenient to hunt till the Water be dried up; for the drops disperse the scent of the Hare, and dry earth collecteth it again.
> The Summertime also is not for hunting, because the heat of the weather consumeth the scent; besides the fragrancy of Flowers and Herbs then growing, consumeth the scent the Hounds are guided by. The best time for hunting with Hounds is in Autumn, for then the former Odours are weakened, and the Earth better than at other time. Here it is to be noted, that they cannot make it so good in the hard Highways as in other places, because they cannot have there so perfect a scent, either by reason of the Tracks or Footing of divers sorts of Beasts, or by reason of the Sun drying up the moisture, so that the dust covereth the Slot. There are other places wherein a Hound can find no scent; and that is in fat and rotten ground, and it sticketh to the Foot of the Hare, which is call'd Carrying, and so consequently she leaves no scent behind her.

We take for granted the deficiencies and difficulties in seeing, for example we ignore the fact that we cannot see through a brick wall, or in fog, or at night; that shadows and lack of contrast make vision more difficult. We overcome these difficulties in seeing, and likewise a well-trained dog overcomes his difficulties in scenting. When on a hot, dry day or because of the irregularities of the ground he finds scenting difficult, he will work closer and more slowly, seeking out the likely patches and difficult cover.

It is interesting to note that an elephant has a far more sensitive nose than a dog. A moth can scent it's mate in favourable conditions up to two miles and even a man can smell .000,0004 mgm. of a scent in one litre of air, and even less than this actually reaches the scenting area in his nose. The dilution of the scent that a dog can appreciate must be many times smaller than that of the man—a really fantastic sensitivity. Bearing in mind the differences between air and ground scent, it is much more likely that your dog will find if he lifts his head and sniffs the wind than if he snuffles along the ground.

As we do not carry a hygrometer and differential thermometer in our pockets it comes about that when in the shooting field we cannot always determine the scenting conditions, and so we still echo the huntsman's words, 'Eh, but it's a queer thing is scent.'

*'It is certain that a good dog
cannot be of a bad colour'*

4 On choosing a puppy: its housing and management

To breed successfully is extremely difficult; if it were not so we should all breed champions. However, the laws of heredity give us certain pointers which must be obeyed. In the wild state only the fit survive and probably an average of sixty per cent of baby animals succumb during their first year. We, however, have to depend on carefully selected breeding.

In wild animals, too, the mother and father train their babies, and the babies also learn from playing with their brothers and sisters. It has been shown that there are periods in the life of a baby animal when he is capable of learning certain lessons. If these periods are missed, the lesson is never properly learned—for instance, a baby duck, if prevented from following its mother over a certain number of days after hatching, will never learn to do so, and a child who is prevented from hearing speech during his first three years of life will never learn to speak properly. A puppy which has been segregated in kennels for the first six or nine months of his life starts at a disadvantage from which he may never recover. If the breeder owns the bitch, the puppy should be allowed to run with his mother; he will come when she is called in, or splash in the river when she is out swimming, and of course all puppies should be taken into the home to play with the children.

On line-breeding, inbreeding and outbreeding

The breeder must differentiate between line-breeding and inbreeding. In the latter characteristics may be strengthened too much, bad as well as good ones. Thus, line-breeding is considered as not closer than half-brother to half-sister, uncle to aunt, or granddaughter to grandfather.

Inbreeding is successful with racing pigeons, which in some cases have been inbred for twenty-five generations, producing champion birds with wonderful homing instincts, fast and strong in flight and with the intelligence to navigate storms. This is true because of the number of birds who either do not arrive home or are culled for late arrival. There is, therefore, a very strong natural selection and survival of the fittest factor. If, however, faults have been acquired in a line through inbreeding or other factors, outbreeding may be tried, but this is a pure gamble as the chance of the mating matching up in other characteristics is very small. Even as regards the fault for which the outcross was made, puppies may inherit the wrong characteristic. However, once fresh blood has been introduced it is strongly to be recommended that breeding back into the desired line should be undertaken at the second generation. Never breed from a bitch or dog with a severe fault.

There are a few pointers to successful breeding. In any animal the genes are fixed at birth; thus characteristics are only transmitted through the parents—it is the four grandparents who determine the qualities that the progeny will inherit, however humbling this may be to parents, either human or canine. The parents, though apparently magnificent animals, may not be capable, as their qualities are recessive, of transmitting their good characteristics to their offspring. It is therefore essential that the breeder should mate his animal with a proven sire or bitch. A superb bitch or dog may produce poor descendants, and a not so good animal may prove a wonderful sire or dam. A breeder must not breed from parents of opposite characteristics in the hope of averaging out, as some puppies will inherit the dog's characteristics and others the bitch's. Dilution of a required characteristic can, however, occur over several generations, so that it is eventually lost.

Certain faults in dogs are hereditary defects: hardmouth and yipping. Any dog is capable of one or other of these crimes, but if he persists after reasonable chastisement, he should be discarded or sold, probably as a pet or to some member of the shooting fraternity as a rough shooting dog. Such animals should not be bred from. It is because these faults are essentially hereditary that they are considered as major crimes in field trials and the dog is discarded.

In sum, the advice that can really be offered is to try to mate your bitch with a proven sire who matches up with your bitch's pedigree, and then to keep your fingers crossed that the mating will 'click'.

The choice

If you have decided on buying a puppy and bringing him up from five to seven weeks old, the only way to choose him is to look closely at the litter, shut your eyes, put your hand into the squirming mass and pick out the first puppy it grasps. The advice Cox gives is as follows:

> As soon as the Bitch hath littered, it is requisite to chuse them you intend to preserve, and throw away the rest: Some remove the Whelps from the Kennel, and lay them several and apart one from the other; then watch they which of them the Bitch first taketh and carrieth into her Kennel again, and that they take for the best; or else that which vomiteth last of all; Some again give for a certain rule to know the best, that the same which weigheth least while it sucketh will prove the best.

In other words, let the bitch choose, or take the puppy with the best digestion. It is interesting to note, however, that we still prefer the little ones. To a large extent this applies to all puppies in the first year of their lives. Most handlers prefer a wick little puppy, but a puppy's further development cannot be foretold with any accuracy even by the breeder himself, let alone the buyer who only sees the dog for a short time. The best advice is 'buy a well-bred puppy from a reputable breeder'; this gives you a chance but no more.

The first decision to make is whether it should be a bitch or a dog. Some people are 'bitch men'—I am one myself and have a much greater affinity with a bitch than with a dog. With a dog I tend to get rather a love-hate relationship and in consequence have not the patience necessary to train him successfully. Most amateurs will find that a biddable little bitch is far easier to handle than a dog, although bitches can be awkward at times, and it is worth putting up with the nuisance of the recurrent seasons. 'Pilling' at the moment is out of fashion and the pills have been withdrawn by the veterinary profession as they are liable to give fits, and also probably increase the number of puppies in the litter, thus possibly causing stillbirths. The position may soon change, however, as there is now a new pill on the market which appears to be much safer.

Your professional, however, with several animals to choose from, generally prefers dogs.

This decided, the next question is to what extent the puppy should be already trained. It is obviously better to buy at about six weeks and undertake the whole training oneself. In that way the training can proceed in an orderly manner and no retraining is necessary. In the majority of cases trained dogs will have no idea of directions or blind retrieves. They will be obedient when out hunting, but will not look to the handler for help and on the whole will be somewhat lacking in confidence. It is very difficult to retrain a dog once he has learned an undesirable lesson. If you have bought a part-trained dog, then it is necessary to spend the next month or more transferring its allegiance to yourself, and then start training in your ways from the very beginning, in the meantime studying and learning the character and abilities of the dog. After you have owned him for a couple of months, it is possible to get down to intensive training.

However, you may choose to buy a fully-trained dog at about two years old and give, say, £700 for the animal. The seller will make an adequate profit; but it is always possible that the dog may have a serious fault—there is nobody who will sell his best dog, so at least go down and see the animal working. Working with dummies is not enough—the dog must be seen working on live game. Such dogs are usually sold as 'seen and demonstrated'. If you can take a friend down with you wise in the ways of dogs, so much the better. Having made your purchase, although he is fully trained, the dog must then undergo at least two months' training at your hands before he is taken out on a formal shoot. He has to get used to your orders and handling, as you have to get used to him. It is not fair on the original trainer to take him home, take him out on a shoot and then because the dog does not come up to expectations ring up the trainer and request that the dog be taken back! After all, you may have ruined by your amateur handling, or rather lack of handling, a particularly valuable animal.

There is the story of the valuable dog sold to America who did not come up to expectations. The new owner got in touch with the trainer and asked his advice. The advice was that the trainer should come to America and stay there for two months, all expenses paid, and that during those two months the new owner must put himself completely at the disposal of the trainer and himself be trained! If I ever bought a fully trained dog I should at least stay a day or two with the owner studying his methods and handling.

Management

The next question is feeding and integrating the dog into

your life and your family's. The ideal food for dogs is without doubt unwashed paunches, which provide semi-digested vegetable residue as well as offal, and somewhat high but not putrid meat which provides easily digestible high-quality protein. Add to this a non-splinterable thigh bone to improve his teeth. Nicholas Cox suggests that when his hounds had killed a wolf, the reward of the dogs was thus:

> When they have bit and shaked the dead Wolf, let the Huntsman then open his Belly straight along, and taking out his Bowels, let him throw in Bread, Cheese, and other Scraps, and so let the dogs feed therein.

However, as these diets are somewhat unaesthetic, I feed my dogs on 'Pal Meat for Dogs' and meal in the afternoon or evening. supplemented in the morning by a light breakfast consisting of the residue of the household milk and a little brown bread. The reason for the light breakfast is that immediately after the meal the dog can be taken out and defecates, thus saving kennel cleaning.

On shooting days or trial days the dog's breakfast is supplemented by a raw egg. One day a week he gets raw meat or liver instead of 'Pal'. If you wish to make the dog thinner you cut down on the meal and brown bread. If you wish to improve his coat you increase the eggs and milk.

Some owners consider that all a dog needs is maize (which is completely unsuitable for dogs), water and dehydrated meat. No doubt a dog considers that he should be fed on pâté-de-fois gras, boeuf Stroganoff and over-ripe Stilton. A dog, however catholic his taste, does not like alcohol unless trained up to it!

The diet of a valuable dog in olden days was as follows:

> Take half a peck of the finest and driest ote meal, and a peck of good wheat; having ground them together, boult the meal and scatter an indifferent quantity of liquorice and anniseede well beaten together; knead it up with the whites of eggs, new ale and barm mixt together, and bake it in

small loaves indifferent hard; then take it and soak it in beef, mutton, veal or venison broth and half an hour after sunrising and half an hour after sunsetting, having first washed and aired your hound, give it to him to eat; this will not only increase his strength but enlarge his wind.

This fine food must have taken a lot of preparation, so we must be thankful for the dog meat manufacturers. Even if there is only one dog in the household, it is a great saving of money to buy the tins wholesale by the case and the meal by the sack. Only a few years ago there was little profit in dogs. Now, owing to inflation, a worth-while living can be made. Kennelling costs £1.30 a day, whilst food costs about 40p. There is little light or heat to pay for so there is a good profit for just feeding and mucking out. A stud fee is £40 and a six weeks old pup whose future is problematical £60.

A likely one year old may cost £300 and a two year old dog trained to hand signals £750, whilst a well trained trial dog costs £1,500 or more. This may or may not be a good thing but it is no use regretting the past. The shooting man must appreciate the amount of work put in to make the dog a paragon of virtues.

A dog should be taken about by his master as much as possible, the minimum requirement being that he should know how to behave in a civilised world, that is that he should be 'pub trained'; and, providing he is not allowed to make a nuisance of himself or lose his training, I allow him in the house. This means that one's wife, and to some extent one's children, must be 'dog trained' and it must be emphasised that if one's wife gives the dog an order she must see that it is obeyed. A dog should never be allowed to pace about but should be put down and made to stay put—this is good for discipline. He should not be allowed on chairs. My dog is allowed on my bed as there is a cover on it. He knows this and when tired of watching television he wisely goes up, lies on the bed and goes to sleep. As one trainer put it 'Have him in the bathroom by all means but teach him that the bath mat is "yours", not "his"!'

When a dog enters a strange room off the lead, he will go round and inspect it for a few minutes before settling down. This, I think, all things being equal, is allowable. I have seen many human beings do the same thing. After that he must settle and stay settled.

On the question of kennels, a kennel should obviously be a dry, warm and comfortable home for the dog. If there is only one dog, electric heating should be installed for use when it is cold in the winter. If there is more than one dog and they can be kennelled together, they will huddle up and keep themselves warm, but when ice is on the ground it is cruel to leave a dog alone in a kennel where he cannot take exercise.

The dog should have a day bench in his run, lifted off the ground so that he can be outside in the day, and the run should have some shade. Inside the kennel his night bed should also be lifted off the ground and have sides about 2 feet high to exclude all draughts. The best bedding for a dog is wood wool—it is clean, absorbent and warm and far superior to straw. There is an old English rhyme about kennels which is very much to the point:

'Life is queer, my masters,
Some people have a bitch without a kennel,
Others have a kennel without a bitch.
How happy is he who hath both a bitch and a kennel.'

Thinking of bitches and kennels, there is one little point worth remembering. If you have, say, three dogs, one dog and two bitches, and one of the bitches comes on heat, if you separate the dog from the bitch on heat by the other bitch, the dog will fret and go off his food and be generally unhappy and lose weight. If, however, you put the bitch on heat next to the dog they will kiss each other through the wire mesh of the kennel and settle down quite happily in domestic bliss.

This line of thought made me think of the copulatory habits of other creatures. The active but cautious earthworm, who always keeps the tip of his tail in the ground in case of sudden attack is as is well known, bi-sexual. Finding their burrows

CHOOSING A PUPPY: HOUSING AND MANAGEMENT

too narrow for amatory exercise, the earthworms come out at night and make love secretly and under cover of darkness. Nicholas Cox speaks of the rabbit as follows:

> When the buck goes to doe he will beat very strongly with his forefoot upon the ground and by that means he heateth himself. When he has buckt, he is accustomed to fall backwards, and lie as if he were in a trance or half dead, at which time he is easily taken.

Before we start on the actual training of our dog, either for the shooting field or for field trials, we must realise that an untrained dog is a nuisance to our host, our fellow guns, and to ourselves. All shooting dogs should be trained to trial standards. After all, a field trial is merely a shooting day with the dogs being judged, and in a trial the basic requirement is that a dog should be steady and find game within a reasonable time, and this is the kind of dog that the ordinary shooting man wishes to own. If we do not instil these qualities into our dog, we shall end up with a half-wild brute which has to be pegged down at the covert side and if sent out to collect a bird will cover half the country and probably end up by bringing back game belonging to a fellow gun. The systematic training of your dog, therefore, is well worth the little extra time and trouble you will have to spend. It is my hope that the following chapters will help you to achieve a dog of which you can be justly proud.

'We were all children once'

5 The first year

For the first six months let your puppy have its puppyhood, playing in the house with the children, other puppies or with his mother, and give him some toys to play with. To a young puppy the world is a strange place and he is frightened at many things. His usual natural instinct, if conditions are disturbing, is either to go home if he is out in the fields or to hide if he is at home. At this stage of his career encouragement, petting and patience are what is required. It is never any use to punish a frightened dog. You could take a month to car-train your dog, but it is essential for him to enter the car willingly. It is no use taking hold of him by the scruff of the neck and pulling him in. The earlier this training is undertaken the less trouble it will be later. If forcible means are used when a dog is frightened it can put him off for a very long time.

There are, however, certain basic ideas that must be remembered. If a puppy does right he must be so exuberantly praised that he will want to do it again.

If he does wrong it must be remembered that he does not

The way to praise   'Come to Mummy'

understand. He is not punished beyond a mild scolding. The handler should be firm, not rough. During the training of a very young puppy, every unpleasant order should if possible lead up to a pleasant one. The rattle of the lead on the table suggests to the dog that he is about to go out. If he is brought home on the lead, he should be allowed a final romp in the garden before he is put into the kennels. It is admitted, of course, that even the best of puppies are unreliable. It may be easier in the initial stages to have your puppy on a cord. It also makes it easier if you have an old dog with you to show the puppy what is expected of him.

The puppy is about six months old and by this time he should know his name. Training begins to teach him to sit (or 'hup'), stay there, come to Daddy, to retrieve a light dummy from a few yards, to heel and to walk on the lead. A small lawn is all that is necessary to train your puppy to quite an advanced stage, even to taking direction signals, and the next few months are spent on these simple commands and exercises. Until these

Training to walk on a loose lead

basic disciplines are firmly instilled, no attempts at further progress must be made; in fact, unless these simple things are well and properly taught no one can begin to handle at all.

One old trainer talks of 'kennel-training', by which he means kennel-yard training. I would go further than this and talk of house-training, and I do not mean the usual thing by this expression. A puppy can be trained very well in the house to sit and retrieve. A narrow passage will prevent him from passing the trainer or running round him. So we advance from house-training to kennel-yard-training, to small paddock-training, and finally to field-training.

1 *To sit*

To train a puppy to sit the word 'hup' is used. It is best to hold its food plate or one of its toys above the level of its eyes. It will

Encouraging a good delivery

then naturally sit in order to recover the toy or food, and the handler repeats the word 'hup'. Soon it becomes automatic —when you raise your hand and say 'hup', the puppy obeys. Do not try to make the puppy sit simply by pushing down its behind—if you do he will raise it. Lift his chin and at the same time push his behind down—he will then sit.

2 *To heel*

In the first instance train with a lead, then without one.

For heeling, a wall may be used or a wire fence or narrow path. Later heeling exercises are taken down on the river bank where temptation abounds. Some of the tricks of obedience training are used here. When the handler stops, the dog is trained to stop immediately. Some training to heel at an early stage is inevitable, but I prefer to leave the tightening up of heeling till later and let it come gradually, the object being to get a free-running dog.

3 *To retrieve*

To train a puppy to retrieve, hold him by the scruff of the neck and throw a light dummy or folded sock a little way away. Release the puppy, and he seizes the sock and plays with it. Encourage him to come near you and when eventually he does so, tickle him.

On no account should the dummy be taken from him—after all, why should he have his new toy ruthlessly taken away? This would encourage hard-mouth and make him unwilling to approach you. After a time he will come to you with the dummy for his tickle, and later, when he is fed up with holding it, he will drop it in your hand. In the same way, when you take the puppy to walk on the lead, take it on and off several times during play but never put him on the lead after play and take him straight home. If you do he will associate being put on a lead with being taken home.

4 *To stay there*

Make your puppy sit for gradually longer intervals, standing in front of him with your hand raised and gradually increasing the distance from him. If he moves, say 'no' and place him back in the sitting position.

5 *To hunt*

During this time you should give the puppy simple exercises in hunting. With the wind blowing towards the puppy, throw a dummy a few yards away. Let him see it thrown but distract his attention so that he does not see the actual fall. This encourages him to hunt for it and use his nose. The puppy will soon understand and can then be started off hunting on completely unseen balls and dummies.

Most trainers stop their dogs from jumping up at them. This is a mistake, and the habit can always be corrected at a later date. The handler wants his dog to come to him quickly

Awaiting instructions

'Out!'

and joyously. One must remember that in all training there is only one bad habit and that is disobedience. If you allow your dog to jump up he thinks it is normal, enjoys it and does not feel he is doing wrong.

Bribes by edible rewards are not necessary and only complicate matters, but you must praise your dog extravagantly. Patience, kindness and firmness are all that is required.

Once your puppy is trained in these simple measures, a few niceties may be introduced. Many trainers, for example, have constructed a collapsible cage or wire partition across their car. This is not necessary—a dog can easily be trained to stay in the back of the car and on no account jump over into the front seat. If he jumps over, push him back and say 'no'. A dog should also be trained not to leave the car until he is told to do so. He may also be trained to wait for us to pass before going through doors—a form of 'ladies and gentlemen first, dogs after'.

The real object of the first year of the puppy's life is not to teach bad habits—fear of bringing toys to master, fear of life in general—to try not to create a neurotic dog but a brave, uninhibited one. But perhaps you don't believe in neurosis in animals? For heaven's sake, don't think that one pat is sufficient—spoil your puppy, praise him for five minutes. It takes a little time to sink in, especially if he is uncertain.

Towards the end of the first year of your puppy's life, obedience has been instilled into him. His food is put in front of him and he will not eat it unless he is told to do so. He will go out and retrieve, a 'seen' retrieve in rough grass, and come romping back joyously to deliver it to hand. By means of gestures—voice and a steady eyeing of the puppy—he has been taught the rudiments of his job and can be trusted at quite long distances, say twenty yards or so, if he is on easy ground. In the last part of his early training the whistle is used, at first combined with the voice and then instead of the voice. He has also been taught to hunt unseen for balls hidden a short distance away. Thus he has become a shooting dog in miniature but has never been asked to do anything very difficult.

'To stroll alone through fields and woods'

6 The training ground—the rabbit pen

All that is necessary for training a dog is a field of short pasture with access to a stream and a small isolated patch of cover. The training grounds that I use consist of twenty or thirty acres of bare, flat field given over to intensive sheep farming, a happy farm where dogs take first place. It is divided into small sections by wire and bounded on two sides by the river, which is about thirty yards across. At one end the river, in a quite extraordinary way, has cut a cliff in the opposite hillside, and it is here that boys help each other down to collect sand martins' eggs. Further along the banks are fairly steep and give a dog experience in entering the water from a poor take-off. A dummy thrown across the river here is difficult for a dog to mark, as he comes down the bank, across the river and up the other side, losing his sense of direction. It is under these banks that the mallards lay and we steal some of their eggs to place under broodies to supply the rabbit pen. Further down again is the beat of the kingfisher, and across the river from here is the plough, useful for retrieves when advanced training has been reached. The kingfisher lays her eggs in a tunnel sloping upwards to prevent flooding. The cock bird is monogamous, although he drives his wife off the beat except during the mating season. To catch fish he dives under the water, catching them crosswise in his beak, never spearing them. He succeeds once in three dives on average. His brood, however, may take up to ten or fifteen dives before they catch a fish, and if they are inept or conditions poor they drown in the attempt.

The only moral that I can possibly derive from this bit of natural history is either that heredity is not enough and must be supplemented by family training, or alternatively that a broken home, even if not permanent, is bad for the children!

Further down still there is an easy take-off and shallow water, useful for training puppies to swim. All along the river bank is a wonderful place for training a dog to keep to heel without hunting, as there are so many smells and interesting places. At the far end of the training ground there is a small enclosed dell with good cover where often pheasants are found. Occasionally we trap pheasants and brail them by cutting their wing feathers to prevent them from flying, again to supply the rabbit pen.

This dell is a good place for teaching a dog to hunt, as it is a small enclosed area which encourages him to hunt in a circle. This is the training ground—the duck on the river, while yellow-hammers and a brace of barren partridges inhabit the centre; rabbits and hares are watched for and used when necessary to tempt the dog, and in the centre is the rabbit pen. For most of training this is all that is required—arid fields, some riverbank and the loan or use of a pen. By using the wind and small irregularities in the ground, by retrieving across a hare or rabbit track, conditions can be made sufficiently difficult for all forms of training except the very advanced. In fact, until the dog is perfectly disciplined too difficult a ground is a handicap. Public parks are no good for training as there are too many distractions in the way of dog smells and people. The greater part of the preliminary training should be done alone.

It is necessary to learn, however, how to use the training grounds. Between retrieves survey the ground and note the amount of pasture, any activity in the way of the passage of farm vehicles or farm life, any heaps of hay to hide a dummy behind or the use of fertilisers or manure to confuse the scent.

You must then decide what kind of dummy to use. It is useless to hide a rubber ball in a hayfield as the dog cannot possibly find it, but it is useful to send your dog after a ball across a path where farm labourers have been working. Balls should be used where the pasture is three to four inches high, otherwise dummies.

The first thing you do when you arrive at the training ground is to let your dog play for a few minutes and let off steam. In the meantime you test the wind yourself and note its direction. While the dog is playing you plan what exercise you are going to give him.

George, the shepherd, is the presiding genius of the training ground, very knowledgeable on horses—the racing variety—and, of course, sheep. He also keeps a keen eye open to see how the dogs are behaving. As his Lancashire accent is the broadest I have ever heard—and I am somewhat deaf withal—there is a certain lack of communication between us, about the same amount as I have with my own dog at times. The other day I enquired after a reckling, a lamb without parents who would not feed with the rest of the flock, whose only friends seemed to be the dogs, a pot-bellied little misery who always seemed to be eating but never put on weight. 'Ah,' said George, 'I scaulpt him and he dee'd.' I had horrible visions of Red Indians when he said that but apparently this particular operation was to crack a thin bone in his skull with his knuckles—perhaps the lamb was hydrocephalic—but I missed him on the next few training sessions.

George says my dog is improving—that is encouraging, as sometimes progress is so slow that you fail to notice it yourself!

The rabbit pen

The rabbit pen is not essential for the training of retrievers. It is a useful piece of equipment and that is all.

Hares and rabbits have been enclosed since Roman times in large vermin-proof parks and warrens. In those days the warrener used to pack wax into the hares' ears so that they would lose their fear of noises and grow fat for the table. The lineal descendent of these parks and warrens is our rabbit pen which is used for training.

A pen for Spaniel training should be very large, but for Labrador work a smaller pen of half an acre is ample. Most amateur trainers will obviously not be able to afford a pen and will have to borrow the use of one from a professional, or perhaps make do with a few pet rabbits.

The pen I use is divided into two by a low fence and gate. At one end there is a swampy pond with rushes, and the whole is situated on a low hillside with ample cover. It is stocked with rabbits, Belgian hares, brailed ducks and pheasants, chicken and an old pet sheep.

Many exercises can be devised in a pen of this kind. A dog can be put down, the chicken collected around him by throwing corn and then they can be flushed and stampeded over him so that he gets used to the noise of wings and is kept steady; or all the animals can be collected in one compartment of the pen and the dog put up at the gate.

Then all the inhabitants can be driven past him—the chicken followed by the rabbits, followed by the ducks and pheasants, and leading up the rear the old sheep—this must be a dog's nightmare. More normally, however, the pen is used as follows: the dog is introduced to the inhabitants until one is quite sure that he is steady. After this very short retrieves are given, the object of which is to make sure that he is not distracted by the many scents and tracks around him and will retrieve the dummy expeditiously. Then longer retrieves are given. Finally the dummy is thrown among the rabbits and the dog has to retrieve from among them. The dog should never be

Steadiness in the pen

introduced to a rabbit pen until his general discipline is assured. Further, it must be realised that a dog soon learns to behave beautifully in a pen but this is no guarantee that his behaviour will be as good when he meets a wild rabbit outside the pen. Rabbits soon lose all their fear of the dog and his trainer, and sometimes it becomes quite difficult to make them run.

One of the advantages of the pen is that it is a confined space in which it is easier to control your dog. Pen work, like all other forms of training, can be overdone. Once your dog has become pen-trained, an occasional refresher visit is all that is necessary. It must be re-emphasised that as in all other forms of training the object is never to let your dog go wrong. It has been known that a dog has been so trained to avoid rabbits and hares that he has refused to pick a dead or bleeding rabbit at a trial, and on one occasion at a trial a dog leapt a fence and landed on top of a hare lying on the other side. The hare made off at great speed. The dog gave a horrified yelp and promptly leapt back over the fence to get away from the hare!

Another test for the pen is to bring your dog up to a brailed duck and let the duck slowly walk away from your dog. This is always a great temptation!

It must be realised, however, that the pen is an artificial bit of equipment with only limited use and cannot and does not compensate for work in the shooting field itself at a later stage.

> *'My object all sublime . . .*
> *to make the punishment fit the crime'*

7 On crime and punishment and the correction of faults

The punishment fit the crime

When a dog is corrected, perfect justice may be administered. There is no question of making an example so that others may be deterred, nor as in human crime must the penalty be made so heavy that the public is protected. Least of all must punishment be administered to satisfy the sadistic irritation of the trainer. The penalty is graded not only by the seriousness of the misdemeanour or crime but also by the sensitivity of the delinquent.

A field-trial champion I knew was so sensitive to rebuke that it was almost impossible to train him with other dogs: if another dog was reprimanded even by change of voice, he cringed and took the punishment to himself.

In nature there are no punishments, only consequences. A dog does not bear malice against his master but learns quickly that such and such an action will bring a corresponding retribution. If, however, retribution does not follow the action he learns even more quickly that he can get away with it. Guilt like malice, is foreign to his nature, so if he is not corrected he will repeat the fault. Here we have established one of the cardinal rules of dog training. However far away the dog is or however hot the day, if the dog does wrong he must be corrected and on the exact spot where he committed the fault.

It is very easy to confuse a dog, and what may be taken for dog disobedience may be only that his little mind is confused.

Jane used to stand on her hind legs and go round in circles yipping when she did not know what to do. Most dogs who are confused either do nothing or go towards their trainer. A dog must be therefore punished immediately he has disobeyed and on the spot where the disobedience took place. It is useless and harmful to discipline your dog five minutes afterwards in a different place. A dog cannot possibly know why retribution has caught up with him!

The list of punishments is as follows:
(1) Scolding your dog.
(2) Flicking him with the lead or dummy string.
(3) Grasping him by the neck and shaking him.
(4) Dragging him to the place of the misdemeanour and shaking him and scolding him there.
(5) Beating him across the back three or four strokes, while holding him by the ruff, with a wide leather strap or rubber tube about two feet long. This last should confined to very *severe* crimes such as running in, crimes which should never be repeated, or persistent and insolent defiance of orders.

After you have punished your dog for a severe crime and given him time for the punishment to sink in, do not forget to make it up with him and take him back into your favour.

Your dog, having been adequately trained and knowing what he is doing, chooses to defy you. He has disobeyed the stop whistle at fifty yards out. You fix the dog with a glassy stare and with ponderous and stately steps advance towards the miscreant, hoping that the youthful self-confidence will ooze from the dog. In due course you arrive at your prey,

CRIME AND PUNISHMENT—CORRECTION OF FAULTS 59

seize him by the neck and, abjuring him in reproachful tones, drag him to the spot where the crime was committed, shake him and throw him on the ground. You then return and in due course either repeat the signal that was disobeyed or call your dog in. This method is far less uncomfortable to the wind and strength of the aged trainer than running out to the place of the crime—in fact if you do so you may find that you are chasing your dog!

On bribery by tit-bits

Most trainers frown on this practice. It must first be clearly understood that it does not matter who feeds the dog—the dog's mind is concentrated on the food and does not project his faithfulness to the man who gives it to him. The dog gives his faithfulness and obedience to and tries to please the individual who gives him orders—his 'pack leader', in fact. If food is given to him as a reward for bringing back the dummy, he may start dropping the dummy to get at the food. On occasion, however, a little judicious bribery is indicated, for example if a dog dislikes getting into a car, he may be fed in the car after he has been persuaded to enter it. This should not be done more than once or twice, and only to make the dog associate the car with pleasure. In the same way training to shot can be carried out at feeding times.

Thus bribery by food should seldom be used but may be tried once or twice, but only if the trainer is in difficulties and wishes to take a short cut.

The correction of faults

Training should always be flexible, that is to say the dog should always be closely watched for developing faults and the training programme altered to correct them. If the dog is sluggish in hunting he may be speeded up with diverse noises and cries of encouragement. Of course, your fully-trained dog will only need the occasional click to start him hunting and to show him that the handler is there. The usual way to correct a fault is to make the exercise simpler or so arrange the exercise that the fault cannot be committed. If a dog on retrieving to hand tends to rush past the handler, retrieves are arranged with the handler's back to a fence so that he cannot pass, and for a time shorter retrieves are given so that the dog does not get up too much speed on the way home.

A method which is described is to lay two sticks on the ground, one on either side of the handler, and then as the dog passes either to right or left, to whip up the stick on that side in front of his nose. I have not personally found this method much use as the timing is difficult—either the dog sees the handler stoop for the stick and does not approach or, as happened with me, I caught the dog by mistake a crack under the chin and for a long time afterwards had difficulty in making him approach me at all.

Another method, and a good one, is to put up your dog—without a dummy—and then, having walked twenty yards away signal him in. When he comes up to you make a great fuss of him, and let him leap up at you. Remember all dogs like being tickled under their chin and it makes them hold their head up.

If a dog tends to circle and not approach the handler or stops a few yards off, the handler may take a few steps backwards or alternatively fall on his knees and pray and cajole the little dog to approach him. It is a fact that a dog will approach a kneeling figure much more readily than a standing one—whether from curiosity and amazement or because a kneeling handler is less awe-inspiring, I leave for the reader to judge, but the main way to encourage a dog to deliver properly is to pat him, make a fuss of him and let him jump up.

If a dog goes out slowly give him short, easily seen retrieves and then short easy unseen retrieves until he is moving well. However, if a dog or the handler is off colour and the training session not going well, abandon it to another day. In the same fashion always end the training session on a good note by giving the dog something that he can do easily and enjoy.

To encourage a dog to go out long distances, lay a double

track by putting the dog down, walking out with the dummy, then dropping it so that the dog can see it, and walking back— so that the dog follows the scent of his master. Later a few very long unseen retrieves are given to the dog, as will be explained in the training chapter. It is emphasised again that if the dog becomes disobedient at this distance the handler must go out to him and shake him.

Hard mouth in a dog is in most cases hereditary, either because it is inborn or owing to the temperamental instability of the animal who bites through excitement; and nothing can be done about it. In some cases, however, it is acquired, as in the case of the old dog who becomes hard-mouthed, or the young dog who has been allowed to collect a running cock pheasant and has been scratched by his spurs. If ever after he is put on a runner, he will give it a squeeze to kill it before he retrieves it to hand.

It is useless in trying to cure hard-mouth to give the dog uncomfortable things to carry. I suppose that all dogs at some time in their career pinch a bird. However, if the fault is repeated, one should get rid of the dog.

Soft-mouthed dogs sometimes drop the dummy or bird on the way back. This is allowable only if he puts it down momentarily to get a better hold. If the dog does this several yards out he should be firmly told 'bring it on'. If, however, he drops it at the handler's feet, the handler should pick it up, throw it out a few yards and tell the dog to fetch it again, and then make a great fuss of him. The object is to make the dog want to give the dummy to the handler. A dog who drops game some yards from the handler shows a grave fault in training and would be severely penalised in the field.

A dog on retrieving from water very often puts down the bird and shakes himself before delivering to hand. Very few dogs would do this with a live bird. However, as the alternative is for the dog to deliver and then shake muddy water over the handler, there is some excuse for the practice! I try to discourage it by patting in the dog as soon as he gets ashore.

A word should be said about the force method of making

a dog hold a retrieve in its mouth but this is for professionals only and should not be attempted by amateurs. The dog's jaws are opened and the dummy is stuffed inside. The dog will try to spit it out. As soon as he ceases to struggle for a brief moment the command 'dead' is given and the dummy removed; or alternatively the dummy is placed in the dog's mouth and held there and pain is applied. As soon as his struggles cease, so does the application of pain. Apart from the fact that these methods of training are psychologically wrong, as a dog should only be punished if he knowingly disobeys, the necessity for trying this method only proves that the dog has been wrongly trained in the beginning.

A dog who is over-eager and tends to run in must never be given any latitude—he must watch other dogs working but never be allowed to retrieve, except for, say, one retrieve after the session is finished. Thus it is hoped that he will steady down and almost become bored with the training. If, however, he does run in then he must be promptly and severely chastised exactly on the spot, unless he is a very sensitive type of animal, but in any case the punishment must be the maximum for your type of dog. Furthermore, the following day the exact circumstances must be reproduced: taking a friend with you, tie a dead hare with its guts hanging out to a long stout cord (or wire) and lay it on the grass. Attach the cord to a crank and wheel so that the hare can be pulled along through the grass. Crank and wheel can be dispensed with, but do add quite considerably to the speed and 'liveliness' at which the hare can be towed. Your dog is then put to heel, but no other care is taken to control him. You take your gun with you and fire several shots to get the dog excited, finally leading him up to the hare, which is jerked away by your friend. If the dog runs in he is punished, and this is repeated until he is sick to death of the hare and won't go near it.

If a dog has made a mistake and the handler has failed to check it on the spot, the next lesson the following day must be a duplication of the condition that led up to this mistake and then the lesson must be repeated often on successive days.

CRIME AND PUNISHMENT—CORRECTION OF FAULTS

Yipping

If the dog talks he should be rapped with the hand across the muzzle. Yipping and talkative dogs inherit this characteristic. It never grows better but, like all faults, always grows worse unless firmly checked. The dog should never be encouraged to talk in the home. If he does so while being patted or played with, play should cease immediately. In the field it should never be overlooked. There are, of course, degrees of talking—there is the grunt of contentment, the grumbling of love, the yapping of over-eagerness, the mewing of excitement and the yipping of hysteria—however, a dog should be seen and not heard.

Mealtimes are useful for training your dog to silence. If he is hungry he may mew while the food is being prepared. Sit him up, get someone to prepare the food before him and rap him hard across the muzzle if he speaks. When training, throw a dummy out on to the river where the current is strong and where he can see the dummy floating away from him, then fire a couple of shots. Again, if he speaks hit him a rap that he feels across the muzzle and say 'no!'. Repeat this every time he makes a sound until he associates the making of a sound with a rap.

Some dogs mature quickly, others are slow developers. It is sometimes difficult to decide whether the imperfections of your dog are due to under-development or lack of maturity, or plain stupidity, or temperamental instability in a mature dog. This is where the constant watching of the dog helps you to make the decision: as all handlers know, for weeks you may have struggled with a dog and apparently no progress has been made, then suddenly one day you take the dog out and he behaves beautifully, the penny has at last dropped; after which, although there may be minor ups and downs, it is only a question of grinding it in until the lessons are irrevocably learned.

Talking to an obedience trainer who had a good reputation for kindness to dogs, I asked him how he got his results in so short a time with so many dogs. He admitted that he had to do it by firm methods. However, we have all the time in the world and better and more permanent results are achieved by patience and kindness. Our dogs also have to work a long way away from us and use their intelligence while doing so. Remember that we are amateurs and are training for a hobby and enjoyment. If it is necessary to beat or maltreat your dog into submission, you had better take up a different pastime.

So be kindly to your little dog and kiss him when he sneezes he only does it to annoy because he knows it teases!

8 Handling

What are the implements of the art? This is ridiculously simple—no check cords or elaborate apparatus. All the handler needs are two or three leather leads with a chain noose end, as leads always seem to get lost; a silent whistle and a horn whistle, half a dozen rubber balls (as these also tend to get lost, this time by the dog), an old tennis racket and about four canvas dummies on ropes so that they can be thrown a reasonable distance. The dummies should not be too light except for young puppies, and one dummy should be without a throwing rope because in early training dogs are sometimes worried by the rope. Long check cords, 'electronic' collars and such devices are excellent in anticipation but a dog gets used to a check cord and behaves quite differently when free. The 'electronic' collar may have its use in experienced hands for a brash dog when other methods have failed. However, the more you train, the more you realise that there are no short cuts. When the penny has eventually dropped with your dog and a partnership has developed between you, it is not a question of your dog letting you down, but of whether you are going to let him down.

The signals

(1) A hiss—as in Schweppes—means 'if you run in you will get a walloping' or 'for heaven's sake settle'.
(2) To sit—'Hup'.
(3) To stop—a single blast on the silent whistle, the hand raised high.
(4) To come in—a double blast on the horn whistle and pats on the thigh.
(5) To go out—a wave forward.
(6) To go to the right—a wave to the right.
(7) To go to the left—a wave to the left.
(8) To jump or swim or, in fact, to surmount any obstacle —'get over' and a wave forward.
(9) To go into his kennel (or car)—'kennel up'.
(10) To hunt—'Hi lost', and clicking with the fingers.
(11) To hunt faster—various encouraging noises.
(12) To heel—'Heel' and a slap on the thigh.
(13) To sit (when he is out)—'Get up', or 'hup'.
(14) To bring him to attention when he is out and disobedient —'Hup'. What do you think you are doing?'.
(15) To drop the game into the hand—'Dead'.
(16) 'Leave it', 'Bring it on', and 'Get on out' are other useful commands.

Once the dog has learned the word 'no'—the most useful word in training—it should be reserved only for emergencies because if it is used too often the handler has nothing left to fall back on. It is the first word the puppy learns. It has been well ground into him and he will never forget it. The handler, as the dog gets older, must not abuse it and must reserve it for the desperate occasion.

The handler

It is important that the handler be as properly trained as his dog, for they act as a team and many a good dog has lost a stake through the mistakes of his handler. Every signal of the handler must be precise and not repeated. There must be due pause between signals to let the little dog's brain cool down. In the early stages of training words are used as well as signals and whistles, but words are gradually dropped and except in an emergency handling should be silent. If words are used the order is only said once—no vain repetitions, as this teaches disobedience.

There is only one thing worse than a yapping handler and that is a yipping dog. A yipping dog is punished and put out of the stake. A yapping handler is allowed to get away with it, although he is demonstrating his lack of control over his dog—in fact he probably does lose a few marks in a trial. Under shooting conditions he would disturb the game and annoy his fellow guns.

These are the handling signals:

(1) To send your dog out, you first look at him and get his attention. Take the whistle out of your pocket and hold it in your left hand.

Under control before sending out

Sending dog off

Bend your right knee so that it is pointing in the direction in which you wish the dog to go and place it slightly in front of him so that it is difficult for him to go out across the knee. Do this quietly with no hurried movements or stamping, as if you do the dog may get confused. Your dog will be watching you so it does not matter in which direction he is pointing. Then sweep your right hand with fingers spread along the side of the dog and in front of him in the direction in which you wish him to go, at the same taking a step forward with the right foot.

When these exercises have been well learned it will be advisable to make various gestures with your arms, swing them, scratch your head or jump about a bit before sending your dog off. This is to promote steadiness in your dog. After all, some day you will be carrying a gun and shooting over him.

It is also important to bend down and scratch your leg before sending your dog off, to make sure that he does not think that bending down is the signal to go. The dog must not move until your hand is swept past his head, so that he takes the right direction. One handler—and this is an excellent idea—never sends his dog off without touching the dog's head. The dog then learns not to move until he gets this pat, this being the final movement before the sending-out signal is given. All this may seem too meticulous, but the dog gets used to the little ceremony and so is steadied by it and is more likely to go out in the direction you want. The only exception to this is if you are sure your dog has marked the bird, when it is better to send him off immediately from whatever side he is before he loses his mark—but be sure never to walk in front of the dog, since this, too, will confuse him and make him lose it.

(2) To stop your dog when he is out, raise your right hand well above your head and at the same time give a single blast on the silent whistle. Then hold the dog for a few seconds before giving a further order. A halted dog may look around him and not at you, almost like dumb insolence, but he is usually scenting the breeze to try to find where the dummy is. As time goes on he will look towards you more and more.

Left 'Hup' when out
Right Sending forward

(3) To send your dog forward raise your right hand to its fullest extent, push it forward and at the same time take a step forward with the right foot, forcing and willing the dog to go out. Later the forward step is left out.

(4) To send your dog to the right: with your elbow bent at right angles and your right hand at shoulder level swing the hand out to the right and at the same time take a step to the right.

(5) Use the same method but with the left hand when sending the dog to the left. Later, of course, the step is again left out.

Obviously the two movements that can muddle the dog are the forward direction and direction to the right. These signals must be made with meticulous accuracy and the dog must be given much practice in them.

In the early stages of training it is a good thing to follow your dog. If he runs to the right signal him to the right. If he

Left Sending dog to right when out
Right Clicking to hunt

comes towards you, pat your thigh and whistle him in. These measures, combined with the exercises described in the succeeding chapters, will gradually indoctrinate him to the strict obedience of orders.

Hunting

Encourage the dog to hunt by clicking your fingers, at the same time moving your hand in an up and down signal. The right hand is usually used for this, as the whistle is in the left hand and it is easier to click with the right. It is the order to hunt an area. If while clicking you point to the ground the dog will probably look down and hunt close. It is better in the beginning not to give direction signals while clicking. Later the dog may be moved slightly from side to side by clicking towards the direction in which you wish him to travel, but he will only move a few yards in contrast to moving him by a direction signal, when he will move about twenty to thirty yards. At first click frequently; later the time interval between clicks is increased, and finally the dog is clicked only when he lifts his head and looks for guidance.

Retrieving to hand

As young dogs are sometimes loth to approach the handler, a great deal of fuss should be made of the dog when he comes up to you. On no account must you take a step forward, as this makes the dog think you are lunging towards him, and this is a slightly threatening gesture. Sometimes taking a step backwards will encourage the dog to approach. Pat your thigh as an encouragement for him to come up to you, but never take your attention from him until the game or dummy is actually delivered. When he does come up to you, take the dummy away from him after a due pause with your right hand while your left tickles his front. This tends to make the dog throw up his head. Now use the word 'dead' to indicate that the dog should release the dummy. If he tends to hold on to it, press the thumb of your right hand into his mouth, pushing his lips with it, and if necessary pass the thumb towards the back of his throat—this always makes the dog disgorge. Again, after he has given up the dummy, make a great fuss of him and let him jump at you, pat and praise him. It is easy to establish discipline later. When he has had his due measure of praise he is again put to heel and his excitement is gently quelled.

Whether a dog should sit before giving up the dummy is a question on which trainers differ. I think it is good training because by doing it the dog will sit more readily when he is out in the field and wait for a fresh order. However, the main thing is to make him come in readily and happily, and any discipline like stamping the foot or forcing him to sit is bad practice, at any rate in the early stages and even later if the dog shows any unwillingness. The dog may deviate when he gets near you and go towards another dog—this is showing off and a sharp word will arrest it.

Good delivery

When retrieving to hand is established the bird must be taken from the dog's mouth with both hands, since he might drop it, or alternatively it might be alive and flutter off. In the same way the handler now takes a step forward with one foot so as to get hold of the bird as quickly as possible.

Words and whistles

Whistles and actions are gradually substituted for words until two commands are left: 'get over' when any kind of obstacle is encountered from a hedge to a lake (but having said 'get over', you should allow time for the dog to choose a reasonable spot!), and 'no', only to be used in dire emergency and never to be disobeyed. A slap on the leg is substituted for 'heel'.

Of whistles there are two—a sharp blast on the silent whistle to stop the dog, and two blasts on the horn whistle, repeated as necessary, to bring your dog in—this is the 'Come to Daddy' whistle.

There are three tones for speaking to a dog: (1) the caressing tone, to congratulate him and pat him, or to comfort him if frightened, (2) the decisive order, and (3) the scolding tone to punish him. It does not matter what is said. I was petting my dog one day. 'Yavrüm iki gurzüm', I said—'you silly little so-and-so'. This is Turkish for 'my little one', 'my two eyes'.

A friend of mine standing by said, 'He's as daft as a brush'. Why a brush should be daft I do not know.

It is important for your dog to get used to these tones and all orders must be given decisively, willing your dog to obey. If not, he will soon take advantage of you.

The dog has been sent off by his handler, who now assumes the basic crouch, whistle in the left hand at his lips, both arms slightly bent, ready to signal at a moment's notice, eyes staring fixedly at the dog, oblivious to all around him except the progress of the animal, and this intensive preoccupation is kept up until the retrieve is actually to hand. The dog looks at the handler. Immediately the handler springs into action and waves the dog on either to left or right. The dog gets near dangerous cover or temptation arises—a sharp blast on the silent whistle, the hand comes up on the halt signal and the dog is held from the three to five seconds necessary for him to cool down. Then the next signal is given, usually away from the temptation. The dog is now in the area and is clicked to hunt. He finds the game and the handler pats his own leg to encourage him in.

'Handling, my masters, can be an exhausting business,' but not for a second must this thread which connects you to your dog while he is away be snapped, because a dog is always aware of you and relies upon you. If you stop concentrating for a moment he will be aware of it and disaster will follow, as he will go off in any direction he thinks fit.

9 Training

The preliminary canter

The general rules of training are similar to those of a Kindergarten school. It is better to train for ten minutes five days a week than for an hour and a half twice a week, since by the former routine the dog does not have intervals in which to forget his lesson. It is better to concentrate on one or two exercises until they are perfect than to give too many difficult exercises at one time, as this will easily confuse him. When, however, the exercise has been performed consistently right and apparently to perfection, variations may be introduced to demonstrate whether the exercise has indeed been really well learned. Should it prove that this is not so, it is back to the original exercise for the next week or so.

At a training session it is better to perform a few exercises well than many exercises not so well. It is not the number of exercises that counts but how the dog does them. For example in teaching direction signals the dummy should be on a plain field in full sight so that all the dog has to do is to fetch it when the signal is given. In 'unseen' training the dummy should be placed so that if the dog follows the direction signal he will find the dummy immediately and does not have to hunt. In teaching the send-off, seen or unseen, the dummy must be immediately found if the dog goes in the right direction. It is only when all the lessons are thoroughly learnt that combinations of lessons are introduced, and it is only on the very final stages of training that difficult retrieves are contrived.

The dangerous time in training is in the advanced stages when a little lack of discipline may put back progress by several weeks.

When training during the summer months, keep the sessions to the cool of the evening. If a training session is going badly through the fault either of the dog or of yourself, give the dog a very easy retrieve and then take him home.

Keep your dog in the kennel for an hour or so before taking him out training, to make him eager. Give him a run before he begins his lessons and after his lessons have finished put him back into his kennel so that he can think them over.

I must emphasise again that the details are important, for the object is to achieve as near perfection as possible in the minimum time. If the handler does not look at these details, it will be glaringly obvious in the finished product.

Marking

A dog has plenty of opportunities to learn to mark during his training and in his first season, when he sees birds shot all around him. Dogs will even stand on their hind legs in an endeavour to see where a bird has fallen. Teaching to mark usually fails—dogs are either natural markers or the reverse, except in the case of a dog who has been so disciplined that he looks round at his handler on the way out to a mark to see if he is doing right and so loses the mark; but these are dogs who have either been too heavily disciplined or are extraordinarily biddable, and are the exception.

A dog has an astonishing memory for a situation where a

Marking the fall

dummy has been thrown some time previously and can count up to about three—after all he has nothing else to think about. Just occasionally, if there is a meadow handy with long grass, it may be useful to go out twenty-five yards, throw the dummy and see if your dog can mark it under these difficult conditions. However, be careful not to leave a track. You should try him occasionally in reeds. It is a salutary lesson to see how good you are yourself at marking!

The dog should also be given some retrieves in conditions where he is liable to lose his mark—throwing the dummy over a hedge or over a wall. Try a long mark in a potato field. The dog will probably run down the furrows instead of across them and thus lose his mark. After a few tries, however, he will go straight out. Another lesson is thus learnt.

Most dogs tend to over-mark. If the dog does overrun the dummy, he should be checked immediately and recalled to the site of the fall. A distinction must be made between mismarking and non-marking. A dog may go out well but the handler knows he has not marked the fall. In this case the handler should immediately take control and handle the dog to the area. In trials the judge may not realise whether it is a mismark or a non-mark—in any case the handler will certainly lose points.

In a perfectly marked retrieve the handler should give no orders whatsoever. However, if your dog is a naturally bad marker you will try to improve him. The Americans' combined dummy thrower and pistol is useful for this. Not only does it teach the dog steadiness to shot, but it throws the dummy an astonishingly long range. Here it's usefulness ceases—probably a rubber ball and racket are just as good. One of the advantages of the rubber ball and racket is that the ball will bounce and leave a trail which the dog can pick up and follow. Rubber balls are obviously preferable to dummies when teaching the dog to hunt.

In considering our own powers of marking it must be realised that most of us have lost the knack. The real countryman, however, is usually a good marker. His vision is rather like that of his dog—he sees the pheasant running along the hedgerow a couple of fields away or the hare squatting in the plough in the next field. The mid-distance is where his eyes are focussed, not half way across the street in case he is knocked down by an oncoming car. I feel sure that neolithic man could mark well a movement in that distant wood or swamp, but we have long lost the faculty and have to learn it again. I would suggest that when a pheasant falls one can mark it by placing the foot pointing in its direction and estimating the distance out, then by noticing landmarks and finally by watching to see if there is any movement in the crop in case the bird has run. This really is very complicated and mechanical when you think of the dog, who does it all by instinct.

Gun training

Very few gun dogs are gun-shy provided they are introduced to the sound of shot early enough and gradually. For the puppy, when training begins, a gun should be fired off occasionally at a distance of one hundred yards or so and the distance gradually shortened. Obviously gun training of puppies should be done while the dogs are feeding, so that a dog associates the noise with pleasure. Like all other temperamental troubles gunshyness can usually be got over by patience, gentleness and familiarity. It must be remembered, however that nervousness or excitability is not a good thing in a dog and is a different thing from sensitivity, which is desirable as long as the temperament is otherwise cast-iron.

When the dog is quite used to being shot over, the gun can be put away until the time when advanced training arrives, as the sound of the gun makes the dog get more excited. The object of gun-training is to make the dog steady but not to make him associate the sound of the report with a retrieve. However, as in all other training we must always proceed in due order.

A dog is very sensitive to smell, also he is suspicious of strange objects. The first necessity, therefore, is to get the puppy used to the smell of the gun and take it out with you a few times on training walks. He then associates the smell of the gun with you and with enjoyment. First use a walking stick and swing it round until he gets used to the movement. Then swing a gun around so that he gets used to it being waved about and not until then do you start to fire the gun. He then accepts the gun and the noise it makes.

Retrieving game

Some time towards the end of training, fresh but not hot game is used instead of dummies—a rabbit, a pheasant, or a partridge. Pigeons are not used at first as they are not close enough feathered. Neither are woodcock or snipe because they have an unpleasant taste. A trail can be laid later with a dead bird. However, the dead bird should at first be used only a couple of times and not again and again. The substitution of dead birds for dummies is never difficult. If any difficulty is encountered, warm the dead bird in your bosom so that it has your smell about it. This method of making a bird attractive applies, of course, especially to woodcock and snipe. Finally, when you are quite sure that your dog will retrieve all game, shoot live birds in front of him and after a due pause send him to collect them. When he has collected freshly shot game, he is no longer allowed to go out to easy retrieves.

Steadiness

Go and play

If you have one dog it is difficult to make him go and play as he usually keeps near his master, and if you have bought a fully-trained dog it may be unwise to encourage him to go and play as he may lose discipline. However, if you are out with friends and there are two or three young dogs with you, this is an exercise which has many advantages. Clap your hands and wave and say 'go on, go and play'. This lesson is easily learned and is one that is never disobeyed! The dogs will run off and chase each other, hunt about for smells on the riverbank, disappear from view into the next field and thoroughly enjoy themselves. In a short while, however, you will find that they will be back looking for you. While playing like this your dogs get plenty of exercise and it makes them hard. They are usefully employing their noses, and by running up and down the riverbank and splashing in and out of the water they will learn to treat water as just another form of dry land. They will also learn to take precipitous banks and bad take-offs with ease.

No dog should be working under discipline all the time, and by letting him go and play you relax the dog and also get a period of relaxation yourself. While your dog is out playing, a dummy may be thrown which he must ignore. When he is near you, but not otherwise, the stop whistle may be used and he may be called back, put to heel and taken under discipline again.

While the dogs are out playing you can relax and sit down behind a tree. You can then watch your dogs questing for you. I have never known a dog lose discipline through this exercise, for he soon distinguishes between playing and working.

'Go and play' emphasises to the dog that when he is working he is under strict discipline but may enjoy himself at other times.

Clicking in an unsullied field

If you watch a young untrained dog while he is hunting, you will notice that he will go to the fall and hunt around for a short time, but if he does not find he will begin to hunt aimlessly in any direction, possibly becoming panic-stricken and starting to hunt wildly. Finally he will lose interest and follow any interesting scent that pleases him. A trained dog, however, will hunt close to the fall, gradually extending the area of his search. If he does not find he will return to the fall time and time again—perhaps as many as five or six times. He will persevere and will not get excited and lose his head.

I think that to produce a free-running dog, the first major lesson should be in hunting, and during these lessons he should be encouraged to hunt always in a circle—in this way at some time during the search he will automatically come downwind of the quarry. The exercise is carried out as follows:

asking for directions

hunting

he's winded it

Studies in hunting

here it is

choose a quiet corner of a field bordered by stone walls or wire where you hope that the ground is not contaminated by the interesting scent of rabbit or hare and it has only sufficient cover to hide a ball. 'Hup' the dog and cover his eyes. Throw a ball a few yards away from him, sometimes backward sometimes to right or left. Then stand back a few yards from the dog and give the hunting signal by clicking your thumb and fingers and saying 'Hi lost'. The dog may immediately find the ball. This is good; this is quick success. Make the exercise gradually a little more difficult but never very difficult, and by clicking and waving the hand encourage the dog to circle you always in the same direction. He can never get far away owing to the restricted area in which the exercise is practised. When the dog has learned to hunt to the click and circle, practise the exercise on more difficult ground—in a small dell with more cover, but always in a contained area, since you should avoid using the stop whistle. Also you gradually stand further away from the dog. In this way you build up self-reliance, style and perseverance.

One professional remarked on seeing this order being given, 'That's typical. Look at him, waving goodbye to his dog.'

Come to daddy

Once you have taught your puppy 'hup' and 'stay there', you should give him exercises in bringing him in from time to time. First you do so by patting your thigh and giving two short blasts on the horn whistle, then by either the whistle or signal. Finally you walk away from him and, without pausing in your stride or looking back, whistle him in. The puppy may not move. If so, you turn and pat him in, but soon he will answer the whistle alone. As usual you practise the exercise until the puppy responds twelve times out of twelve. Not till then is the whistle used when he is out hunting. However, in this case stop him first with the stop whistle, then whistle and pat him in. Finally, when he is fully trained you can pat him in a short way or bring him right in by using the whistle.

84 TRAINING THE RETRIEVER

He who must be obeyed

The stop whistle must never be disregarded and must be practised endlessly during training. Never use the stop whistle when the dog is on the way in towards you, as this tends to slow the dog up and style is lost. Occasionally use it on the way out to a dummy, but only do this when the dog is thoroughly obedient to it. It is also better until very late in training to avoid using the stop whistle when the dog has winded the dummy, because in a young dog it is almost inevitable that you will be disobeyed. The following story illustrates the value of the stop whistle. Son, who has been training his dog over some months: 'Father, may I bring my dog out shooting with you tomorrow?' Father: 'Well, son, can you stop your dog anywhere and at any time?' Son: 'Yes, father.' Father: 'Then of course you may my boy—you have a trained dog.'

Thus in training never blow your stop whistle twice.

Never blow it when your dog is too far out to obey you.

Down the line

The object of this exercise is to teach the dog to go out in a straight line. Use a wire fence with the wind blowing from the dog to the fence, otherwise he may scent something on the other side of the fence and try to jump it. While walking along the fence you drop a dummy in full sight of the dog. Twenty yards on you 'hup' the dog and then continue walking down the fence. After a short period you turn, pause and give the forward signal to the dog, who retrieves the dummy. The distance between the dog and the dummy remains constant—twenty to thirty yards; the distance between the dog and you is gradually increased until it is over one hundred yards. Later you drop the dummy unseen *and unheard*, for to a dog hearing is almost as good as seeing. Later still choose the open field. 'Hup' the dog, walk out a hundred yards and throw the dummy into the air so that the dog can see it. You then walk back along your own track to the dog and send the dog out. The dog collects the dummy at full speed. Not only does he know where

Find the lady

it is but you have made a double track of your own to the dummy. This exercise (1) increases the dog's speed, (2) teaches him to work at a distance from his master, (3) teaches him to go out straight. Later still, of course, the same exercise is used in the open field with an unseen dummy previously hidden. Be very careful as usual to lay your tracks so that they do not help the dog, either by walking downwind from where the dog is going to work or by hiding the dummy from an entirely different direction from where the dog is.

Find the lady, or the three-card trick

Training is always done at right angles, and the exercise to be described is the primary training exercise. It is performed in one of its many forms in spring, summer, autumn or winter on all kinds of terrain; and whenever discipline becomes slack, back we go to the training grounds to 'find the lady'. In the fully developed exercise you put down the dog facing you. Throw out three dummies meticulously at right angles, one to the right, one to the left and one straight on over the dog's head. You then back and send the dog for the dummy you wish.

At first you should do this with two dummies, staying only a few yards from the dog, and he is always sent for the dummy thrown last. When the dog is completely sure of this exercise, send him for the dummy thrown first. Once this is learned, use three dummies beginning again with the dummy thrown last, and gradually progress until the day you send the dog three times for, say, the left hand dummy. This will tend to confuse him if you now send him for the one on the right. Next place one of the dummies unseen and give him practice in going for this one. While the distance between the dog and the dummies is kept constant, about twenty or thirty yards (or the normal easy throw of a dummy) gradually increase your own distance from the dog until it is again over a hundred yards.

At this point you may introduce other variations: do not back away from your dog but walk straight on and then turn. But in the beginning all movements and placing of the dummies must be accurate and as usual the exercise must be made so

Direction practice

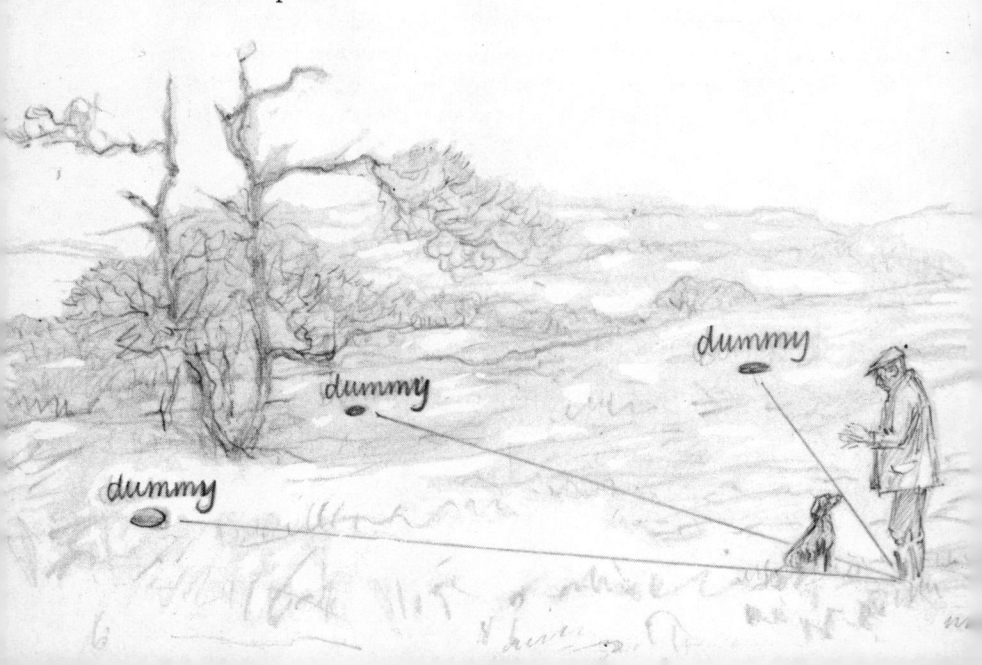

easy that the dog does not make a mistake. If he does make a mistake the exercise must immediately be made easier.

The next variation of the 'three-card trick' is practice in sending your dog out. Sit the dog by your side and throw out the dummies at acute angles, then send him for whichever one you wish.

Gradually increase the number of dummies from one to four and in this way the dog learns to go out accurately and willingly. Again, when the lesson is well learnt, introduce unseen dummies into the game.

Unseen

Introduce more and more unseen dummies, at first without diversion dummies, and watch how your dog works, and then throw in diversion dummies. There are perhaps three ways in which a dog goes out to the area.

A dog going out to an unseen bird may go out straight, looking back every twenty yards or so for directions from his handler until he reaches the area, like this:

Getting into the area of the fall

or better still and showing more style, especially if he is working into the wind, he will go out in zig-zag fashion savouring the wind and hunting all the way.

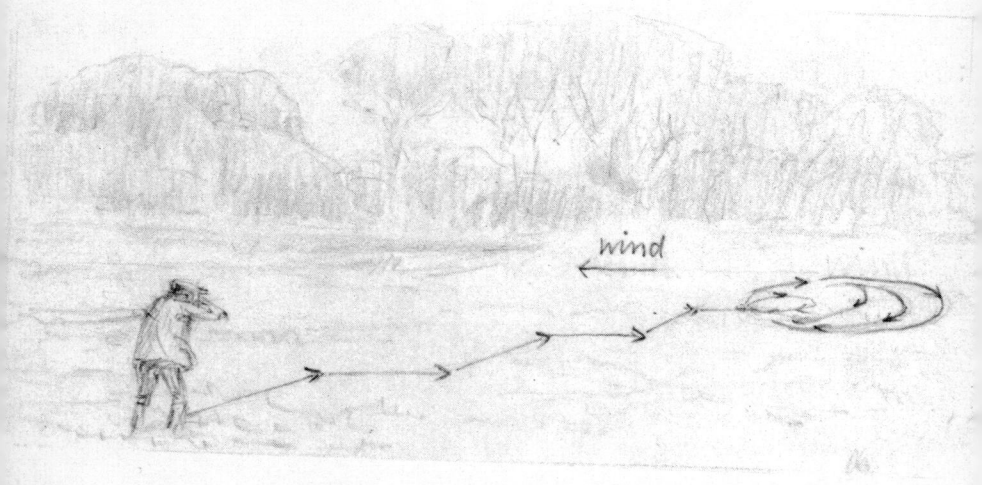

It would be nice to be able to train your dog to hunt an area every twenty yards or so in a circle rather like this, covering all the available ground.

TRAINING 89

Unfortunately, if your basic training hasn't been adequate your dog is likely to go out like this:

Explanation

The dog was rather badly sent out too far downwind and drifted with it. An effort was made to correct this and straighten him up and he responded well, but the handler managed to get him too far upwind and when pushed forward he passed the dummy upwind of it. In spite of every effort to stop him and click him to hunt, he ran on to the hedge and started to hunt this upwind. He was called back away from the hedge and obeyed, but went rather too far again. He was clicked to hunt and did so but was not really in the area, so had to be pushed out. He then winded the dummy and collected it. The retrieve was made but no medals could be given.

The real test of your success as a handler is how your dog goes out and works to unseen dummies with diversions. If he goes out confidently and looks to you for directions which he obeys, and perseveres in his hunting, you have completed his training. That is why advanced training consists of nothing but virtually unseen retrieves.

You can tell when the dog is ready for advanced training. For weeks you have been training your dog. Sometimes he is improved but sometimes your training has not been quite so successful. Then suddenly all the training you have given him seems to click. One day he is a rather erratic youngster, the next he is apparently a quite well-trained dog.

It is encouraging sometimes to think of this when you are struggling to teach him the basic principles and they are not apparently sinking in or being remembered. Sooner than you think you will suddenly realise that he has learned them all.

BASIC APHORISMS or—THE SAYINGS OF ATKINSON—to be remembered throughout training and afterwards.

(1) A dog is a precision instrument—be careful not to blunt it.

(2) Always make the dog sit when you put him up either when he is near you or out in the field. This makes it more difficult for him to run in or, if he is out in the field, gives him time to pause if he is tempted. It also looks more stylish.

(3) Although there is no rule about walking to heel and in shooting country a dog has to follow as best he can, he should be trained to walk on the left side and with his handler. It is a nuisance if the dog dodges from side to side behind you and the handler does not know where he is.

(4) Hunting at heel must be prevented at all costs and is easily done by a flick of the dummy cord whenever the dog begins to do it, either on your thigh or on the dog—the latter is the less painful!

(5) Always 'hup' the dog before giving another direction signal. Then pause for at least three seconds to let your little dog's brain cool down, before giving the next order.

(6) The object of training is to build up the dog's confidence in himself and to teach him that his master is always right. Your dog must therefore never have a failure. The

TRAINING 91

reverse of this is also true. The object of training is also to build up your confidence in your dog so that you know he is always right. He should therefore never have a failure. If he fails to find the dummy, another must be dropped without him seeing it so that he can find it easily.

(7) All exercises must be made so simple that the dog can perform them—the object of training exercises is not to correct him when he goes wrong but never to let him go wrong. It is, therefore, necessary only to increase the difficulty of the exercise very slowly indeed.

(8) No exercise must be abandoned until the dog is right twelve times out of twelve. If this is not observed it will be found that the time that the dog lets you down is when he is under pressure in the field. To eradicate a fault is far more difficult than to prevent one occurring. It is, in fact, easier in many ways to train a dog from the beginning than to take on a half-trained dog which has already learned undesirable lessons.

(9) Remember that your dog is running a hundred yards but that you have stood still. Give your dog adequate rest between retrieves.

(10) Do not teach disobedience. Never give an order when your dog is so far out that you think it might be disobeyed. When your dog stops and looks to you for help, you are nearly there.

(11) A dog can always be stopped but you cannot always make him go. The object is to produce a free-running dog. It is very easy to curb enthusiasm.

(12) A dog should steadily improve in the course of weeks. If he does not or gets worse, look and see whether you are at fault. Perhaps you have unconsciously altered your signal and are confusing the dog, or giving him exercises that are too difficult. Perhaps you are giving the dog too much freedom or alternatively are disciplining him too much. The observer can often spot where you are going wrong when it is difficult for you to spot it yourself.

(13) When a dog is out working there is a thin thread

between you and your dog—be careful not to snap it. For instance, if your dog looks to you for a signal you must give it to him immediately, otherwise the dog will look away and do what he thinks best. He will no longer be in touch with you. If you lose concentration when he is out, you will miss the opportunity to help him when he needs it most or is getting into trouble. If he is at heel and you fail to concentrate on him be sure that he will know it and lose discipline.

(14) Trust your dog. This aphorism is the one above all others to be remembered in advanced training and trials. The dog goes out of sight—there is nothing you can do and you should not get worked up and excited. If your dog is good and finds himself at fault he will immediately come back to you, and when fully trained he will not go off on a hare trail or out into the blue. If you cannot trust your dog he should not be out with you in the shooting field. If your dog has been properly trained and is level-headed he will do his job, unless he is stopped from doing it by unnecessary interference from you. The dog knows far more about what is happening out there than you do. Anyway, if he cannot find he will either ask you for help or automatically go back to the fall and start again.

> Irrational, did I say? I may mistake if what Actiarius reports be true, who thought dogs have reason, and use logick in their hunting; for they will cast about for the game as a disputant doth for the truth, as if they should say, the hare is gone either on the left hand, the right or straightforward; but not on the left or right—therefore straightforward: whereupon he runneth forthwith after the true and infallible footsteps of the hare.

(15) Most handlers will agree that your mood communicates itself to your dog and the handler who keeps calm and collected will achieve the best results. It is also certain that a dog is quite capable of spotting inattention and what is more will take advantage of this. This is very evident if you carry a gun in the shooting field and become absorbed in the shooting or neglect the dog.

(16) The best dog requires the least handling. He makes the finding of game look simple and easy.

(17) Never whistle your dog when he is out of sight unless to recall him. This may appear obvious but is very easy to do in rough cover. The dog may only appear for a second or two, and if you fail to stop him in that second he will be behind a tree and not able to see you. If you are worried and your dog is out of sight, click your dog. This will reassure him and in due course he will reappear.

(18) Never whistle your dog when he is out of control—in training this teaches disobedience.

(19) Whip your dog once and he will, if the whipping is justifiable, obey and become your slave. Continue to whip him and he will become a hardened criminal who will behave worse and worse.

(20) 'A fast dog has a good nose—a dog can only go as fast as his nose'—now where does this lead us to? A young dog will overrun the scent through enthusiasm. Later, however, when he has learned to hunt and use his nose, he will moderate his pace to his scenting abilities, and we usually find that a fast trained dog has a good nose.

(21) If a dog is frightened, it is not enough to pat him 'good dog'. At least five minutes must be spent in patting and caressing him until he has forgotten his fears. After all, you don't just pat your child if he has had a nightmare. You take time and trouble consoling it and possibly let the child get into bed with you.

(22) In difficult country it is far better to place your dog twenty yards downwind than one yard upwind.

(23) Remember that when your dog is in his kennel, he can neither be acquiring bad habits nor learning to disobey.

In case I have confused you by the erudition here displayed, let me gently suggest that in the ensuing years of training dogs the truth will become apparent to you.

One last aphorism—you are far more intelligent than your little dog, so use your low cunning to persuade him to follow out your ideas rather than his own.

10 Obstacles and how you hope to surmount them

Considered in the broadest sense there are many things that distract a dog or prevent him from reaching his quarry. That interesting hare track which crosses his path, that bunch of nettles which stings his nose, or that small gutter with brambles on the other side into which quite reasonably he doesn't wish to jump! The handler must therefore try to visualise what is happening to hold up his dog. Certainly if he sticks on the hare track, this is defiance and he must be ordered on at once.

Once, when we were training some dogs and I sent one of them across the river, he stuck on the other side and was recalled. Another dog, a field-trial champion, was sent—he, too, was rather sticky but collected his dummy. Later we found that the otter hounds had killed the night before and the otter had been broken up at that spot. What a feast of smells—man, dog, blood, and otter! It is, of course, for this reason that training is undertaken well away from woodsides or other delectable places until strict obedience has been achieved.

The dog must be accustomed to animals. This is easy with

sheep, and after due time a dog should be able to retrieve a dummy from among them, always remembering that the farmer does not like the sheep disturbed, especially before and during the lambing season. It is rather more difficult to accustom dogs to cows, and great care should be taken with bullocks because if one of them chases and tups your dog, it may get badly hurt and in any case will be permanently frightened of them. Perhaps it is best only to watch bullocks from the other side of a hedge!

Jumping is taught by beginning with very low, solid jumps and by example, preferably the example of other dogs; but if dogs are not available you can set the example yourself. After the dog has mastered a low wooden fence he is introduced to wire, first jumping as his master gets over the wire and then after a dummy. Let it not be thought that the lesson ends here—one lot of wire can be very different to another in both height and appearance. Also there are two ways of jumping wire: running at it and leaping it clear, and cat-jumping it. It is very possible that on a shoot or a trial the take-off can be so bad that the dog has to cat-jump it, so experience in both types of jumping must be given.

As in all training, as far as possible, jumping must be made into a game, and if you sit on a low wire fence the dog can be made to jump backwards and forwards and enjoy the exercise. The dog may well leap a fence but, having retrieved the dummy, may run up and down seeking an easy way back. At the beginning it may be that he does not like jumping with the weight of the dummy, or that he thinks the wire too high for him. Of course this shows intelligence, but is decidedly sloppy and should be checked. He should be halted and then taught to leap the fence with the retrieve.

At a working test, one of my dogs who had done an excellent retrieve started to do this. I thought to myself 'Silly little bastard'. Unfortunately, I quite inadvertently voiced my thoughts out loud and a friend of mine in the crowd called out to the judge, 'Disqualify him, judge! He has used bad language.'

Jumping a fence

Cat jump

Well over, hind legs well up to avoid the wire

The same rules apply to swimming. At first the puppy is coaxed into the water a few yards after another dog or a dummy floating near the bank. Later he starts swimming with amateurish splashing but soon learns to swim efficiently. The next lesson he has to learn is to make the best use of and swim with the current. Following this he is taught to retrieve a dummy in the river from a bad take-off, and finally a dummy is floated far down river and the dog is allowed to swim after it to obtain length.

Introducing the puppy to water

Encouraging him in

Going out to retrieve across water

OBSTACLES AND HOW TO SURMOUNT THEM 99

If you give your dog the 'go and play' exercise near the riverbank, he will soon learn to play in the water and out of it, treat water as if it were dry land, scramble up and down the most difficult banks and even dive into the water. A trained dog, as is well known, will follow under the water a wounded duck which is diving.

Once the river has been conquered, let lake swimming be considered. While the dog will swim out into a lake after a seen dummy, it is another problem to persuade him to swim out into a large area of water unseen, so he must be given experience of large areas of water. At the same time he may be given practice in taking direction signals on water, and diversion dummies should be thrown. Training on the river should be combined with training on a lake, as it is difficult to perform water-handling unless space is available. Early lessons in swimming should be undertaken in the summer. Later on the dog will go into the water of his own free will on the coldest days.

When you have trained your dog to retrieve across water seen and unseen, the next exercise is to place your dummy across water, but away from the opposite bank, as the dog is loth to leave the bank when he is across. It must be appreciated, however, that as the dog is out of reach once he is across the river, all such exercises must be undertaken with discretion.

Let us consider the older dog who is frightened of water and see how we can surmount this obstacle. It is as well to go for the lesson with as many friends and dogs as possible. Then take the dog by the waterside and make him sit, in the meantime letting the other dogs play and splash in the water. When he gets excited, place the dummy a couple of yards into the water where it is shallow and encourage him to get his feet wet. If this fails, walk into the water but don't call him—make encouraging noises, to build up the excitement as much as possible. If the try is successful and the dog enters the shallow water, after a time place the dummy a little further out until eventually he has to swim a few yards. If this is not successful, you can cross to the other side of the river and then

Retrieving unseen across water

walk further and further away, calling your dog all the time. He may brave the river to catch up with you. If this again is not successful, the lead may be used but it is only to give the dog confidence. It must always be left slack and never tightened, and if the dog backs away from you it must be dropped. This sometimes works because the dog feels more confident when he is attached to his master by the lead. Finally, when the lesson has been successful, it should be repeated the following day, and at frequent intervals thereafter until full confidence is achieved.

Some dogs enter water by jumping far out. Some dogs run into the water, while others choose their spot of entry with

'Hupping' dog across water

care. How a dog enters water is not important so long as he does it willingly. However, give him time, whether it is wire, a wall, a runnel, or a river, to make up his mind about the best way of encompassing the task.

To surmount a wall the dog runs up it, balances on the top and then drops down on the other side. To see a small border sheepdog do this is to me an incredible sight, as the dog is so completely dwarfed by the height of the wall. Many shepherds train their dogs by leaving them and walking away, but this is not necessary or advised. The dog as usual is trained either by watching the sheepdog or by giving him a low wall to surmount, or climbing backwards and forwards over a wall

Wall training

yourself! I have found this last method very strenuous after performing the feat about a dozen times! Drystone walls are rather insecure and care must be taken that the wall you make your dog scramble over is a secure one. However, it is usually quite easy to make a drystone wall fit the dog by removing stones during initial training.

Facing cover

Labradors, unlike Spaniels, are not really good at facing cover. Nor should 'tiger' country be introduced until advanced

Success

training is reached. A good exercise for your dog at a later date is on the shooting field. Allow him to follow you whatever the difficulties, and never help him or find him an easy way, on the principle that where you can go, so can he.

A hedge is, of course, another obstacle. Exercises must be given in pushing your dog through a hedge and out on to the field on the other side. Of course, he will prefer to remain along the hedge bottom. The main difficulty here is that the dog is liable to disappear from view. He must therefore be pushed through the hedge, held immediately and then pushed out into the field while the handler still has a chance to see his dog. The dog must have experience with as many and varied conditions as possible.

'Ha,' said the teacher, 'do you know you haven't spoken to your dog once in the last half hour? Either you or your dog must have improved'

11 Advanced handling

At the beginning of training words were used to teach the dog. These, as has been pointed out, are gradually dropped and signals and whistles used almost exclusively. Now, in the advanced stage of handling, the signals and whistles themselves are largely discontinued. The dog is obedient and knows his job. He is 'frozen' to his handler and looks to him if he is in difficulty. If he goes out of sight he will come back and have a look at the handler to ask him what to do next. He can be trusted to ask his way to the area and to remain in the area when he gets there. Any unnceessary signals merely distract him from his job, and the handler should watch until the dog demands further directions.

When the dog has reached this stage any retrieve is made to look easy. Thus we have now gone the full circle—in the beginning the teacher instructed the handler and the handler directed the dog and gave the dog praise if he did well; now the dog asks the handler for instructions and the handler turns to the teacher for praise!

Off to a marked retrieve

On a marked retrieve the dog will go out in a rush. Woe betide the handler who whistles unnecessarily, for the dog may not obey him! When he is hunting an occasional click, but only when the dog looks at you, is all that is necessary. If the dog is out of sight, an occasional click to reassure him should be given. Only if the dog is going wrong must the stop whistle be used and direction signals given.

On an unmarked retrieve because well-trained dogs will always hunt back towards their handler or can be brought back towards the handler, it is good practice, ignoring wind, to push your dog out beyond the dummy. If the dog fails to find it on the way out he has a second chance on the way back. On the other hand, if a bird has fallen in thick cover where you will lose sight of the dog, it is better to stop your dog and tell him to hunt before he has reached this cover rather than to send him forward into the blue where he may markedly overshoot and you will not be able to direct him. Always remember that he will hunt in a circle of, say, twenty yards and return to where you first told him to hunt, or at least come back and look for you. It is, of course, usual to push your dog out so that he hunts downwind of the dummy. If, however, there is a strong wind blowing, because dogs do not like facing a strong wind and drift with it, it makes sense to send your dog upwind so that when he has been pushed far enough out he will have drifted down and arrived in the area. Similarly, in all difficult conditions of the ground—for example, pushing your dog out of roots on to a plain field—it is best to play him out in small runs, using the stop whistle, and then push him a little way, stop him again and push him out again, thus keeping full control of the dog. However, in normal circumstances it is a mistake to use a stop whistle too early as a dog must be allowed to get going and the less the handler interferes with his dog the better. The handler must always be on the look-out for trouble and prevent his dog getting into it, stopping him before he reaches that fence or rough areas where unflushed pheasants may be lying.

Certainly in the shooting field and quite often in trials it may be necessary to handle your dog in conditions where he cannot see you. When your dog is almost fully trained, such conditions can be simulated in practice by using walls or hedges or handling in woods. The emphasis here is on 'fully trained'. Such advanced exercises should not be attempted with a young dog. In these circumstances you have to wait for his reappearance, immediately giving him a direction signal when he does so. Sometimes there is a deathly hush and the dog fails to reappear for what seems to be aeons of time. All the handler can do is to repeat to himself that Russian rhyme which goes something like this:

'Doggie, doggie, where are you?
Drinking vodka up a tree'

—and hope for the best.

A handler must be able to hold his dog in a very small area. The handler can see where the game is but there is no scent. He handles his dog to within a few yards of the game and clicks him to hunt. Every time the dog tries to hunt wide he will use the stop whistle to bring him back into the area and then click him again. If the dog has been properly trained he will eventually either see or catch a whiff of the game.

A dog may put up a hare, rabbit or pheasant even on the way back. Therefore the handler must never relax until the bird is in the hand. He must always be ready to call the dog in, or in an emergency shout 'no' if he veers towards the game.

At times most handlers lose control of their dog. It is no use shouting and whistling and advertising to the world what has happened. Gamesmanship is now necessary. Your dog will no doubt circle. Wait after that first whistle which he has disobeyed until you think he will react. Whistle again and perhaps say 'hup', then pause for a long time before you start handling him again.

In handling you must never get excited or flustered. Give all commands forcefully, willing the dog to obey, and then give him plenty of time. The dog will respond to this treatment.

If a dog goes out crooked, straighten him up at once. The further out he gets the more difficult it will be to correct the bad start.

In all handling you must remain still—there is a tendency to take steps forward. This does not help your dog—in fact he looks back to the position where you were standing and this may confuse him. In like manner steps should not be taken to one side or the other. If you lose sight of the dog it is better to wait for him to reappear than to alter your own position to see him. Move only if there is something obstructing your vision. In advanced handling the handler should always seem nonchalant, relaxed and carefree even if he is not!

The following are three examples of difficult retrieves. In the first the pheasant has fallen under a high bank with the wind blowing up the bank. The handler will best make the retrieve by sending the dog along the top of the bank. In the

Getting dog down wind

second retrieve (see p. 110) the bird has fallen in a narrow ditch, and, of course, it follows that there is no scent. The dog will want to jump the ditch and not go down into it. He must therefore be held steady and for an appreciable time on the edge of the ditch and signalled to hunt by clicking downwards. If a pheasant lies in the open on the edge of a ditch or rough ground and your dog has been placed near the bird but does not wind it immediately, hold him and then move him on to the pheasant—but do not click him to hunt, or he will immediately hunt the rough ground and miss the pheasant lying on the plain ground.

The following descriptions are of two typical examples of advanced handling, one on a marked retrieve, the other on an unseen one.

(1) The bird is shot and even before it has fallen the handler has looked down at his dog to note his steadiness and whether he has marked the bird. Simultaneously he has himself tried to mark the fall of the bird and decided whether it is a runner

Retrieve from a narrow ditch

or not. He has already noted the direction and strength of the wind in case this knowledge is required later. He immediately sends his dog out without moving and without ceremony so that he will not make the dog lose his mark. The dog probably goes out in a rush. By the way the dog goes out the handler decides whether the dog has in fact marked the bird. If he has not he treats it as an unseen retrieve. The dog reaches the area, and starts to hunt. After a time he may leave the area, and the handler has to decide whether the dog has taken a true line or is perhaps wandering down a hare track. If the handler decides the dog has not taken a true line, he is called back and handled on to any ground in the area which he has not covered. If, however, the dog looks as if he means it and takes a true line, the handler will have his suspicious confirmed that the bird is a runner and on no account call him off, however far the line takes the dog and even if unseen game is disturbed.

There always appears to me to be an undue number of runners in field trials, partly because the guns may be somewhat nervous of shooting before an audience, and partly because most of the birds are shot up the rear. It is also impossible for the handler, whose primary duty is to keep his dog steady, to be sure whether any given bird is a runner or not.

(2) The unseen retrieve is handled quite differently. The handler having been given the mark and satisfied himself that he knows it and will not lose it, considers whether the bird is a runner. He then studies the ground and looks for possible dangers, and decides not only the best route to send his dog but whether to send him out freely or in short runs. With all due ceremony he sends the dog out, moving him before sending him out if the dog has seen another bird fall so as to distract him and take his mind off the seen bird. He also moves his dog away from the guns and beaters, so that the dog can see him well and will not be distracted on his return. He has thus done everything in his power to send his dog out accurately.

The dog is allowed to get going and then, if slightly crooked, is straightened up and handled into the area. The area obviously varies according to the type of country and scenting conditions, and in good scenting conditions, with the cover not too thick and a moderate breeze, it could be a point with a forty yard radius. In bad scenting conditions the area must be cut down. Again, if the dog takes a line and means it, there is a suspicion that the bird is a runner, and the dog must be left alone and then all the handler can do is pray. If the dog is called off he will not take that particular line again. If in hunting the dog lifts his head and turns, even if he is at the edge of the area he should be left alone. Perhaps he has had a scent of the bird. Then if he starts hunting close he should not be given any further orders but allowed to puzzle out the problem himself. If, however, the bird is in full view of the handler—e.g., half submerged in a stream—the handler must be prepared to hold his dog at the spot until eventually either the dog has a slight whiff of the bird or sees it.

If the handler has to follow after other dogs, the tactics are a little different. First play your dog in the area to demonstrate your complete control of the dog, then cast your dog in a wide area and let him follow any line he chooses to take. After all, if good dogs have searched the area it is reasonable to suppose that the bird has moved or is down a hole.

In any case, after the preliminary demonstration far more latitude must be allowed. The wounded bird can, of course, run in any direction and I have seen them picked much nearer the guns than the fall. This must be worrying for the handler; as he had to see his dog hunt back almost to his heel.

If while out hunting seen or unseen, the dog puts up a hare or a rabbit, he is immediately stopped by a loud 'no'. Having obeyed the signal, the dog must be moved from temptation a very considerable distance. After adequate pause to forget about the hare, he is worked on to the area again. If this is not done he may swing back on to the hare track instead of obeying the handler's orders. Similarly, if the handler wishes to collect one of two pheasants that are down, the dog should be handled away from the unwanted one and then brought round on to the other. The handler's job is to keep his dog out of temptation, to help him without worrying him so that he can be free-running, and never to let him get out of control.

Then there are three more retrieves:

The birds on the left and right are dead and lying on open ground; the centre bird is a runner. It is vital to collect this one first. Let the dog out in short bursts. When he has retrieved the bird, whistle and pat him back.

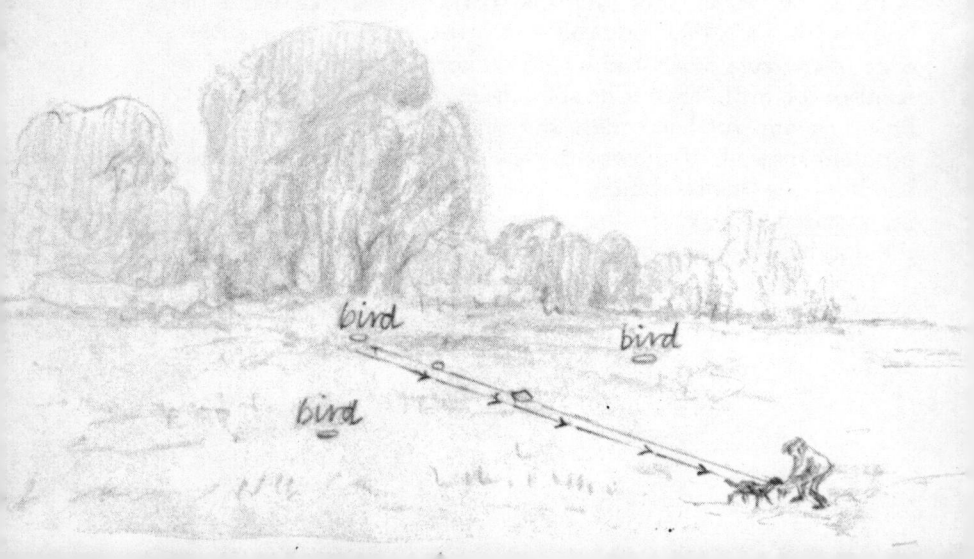

ADVANCED HANDLING 113

The handler often has to direct his dog in kale, bolting beet, commercial Brussels or high mustard, where it is impossible for the dog to mark or to see the handler when he is out, and also impossible for the handler to see the dog to direct him—the only indication he has of your dog's position is the movement of the crops. This naturally makes handling very difficult.

First clear a space for your dog and yourself and then send him out meticulously towards the fall, taking note of the wind and setting your dog slightly upwind as he will tend to drift downwind. The dog will not run out his usual twenty to thirty yards but will tend to want directions sooner, so you should order him by voice to 'get out' at fairly frequent

Voice must be used—'Get on, get over, get on out'.

intervals. When he arrives at the area, order 'hi lost' and click to hunt; if he goes too far you must, of course, recall him; in these difficult conditions a dog will tend to hunt more widely, and may even lose his sense of direction and have trouble in returning to you on completing the retrieve.

'Keep your dog away from temptation.' The handler must not let the dog jump down the bank on to the rough ground

'Unseen, unseen, unseen'

12 Advanced training

When your masterpiece has finished his initial training the polishing process begins. Now is the time to arrange the difficult retrieves. Place the ball out on a plain field or in a hollow with your dog working from roots, or conceal it cunningly under a bank with the wind in the wrong direction, or put it behind a tree. Now is the time to train your dog in 'tiger' country, stinking and heaving with game!

In these new and difficult surroundings the dog may display his worst characteristics. Disobedience must be dealt with immediately by a scolding or a shake as usual and no misdemeanour allowed. However, if things do not rapidly improve, take the delinquent back to the arid training ground with a wild cry of 'back to barracks!', and institute a further course of 'find the lady'.

It is a great temptation to begin advanced training too early and the only result is disappointment. From now on very nearly all retrieves should be unseen. At first it is as well to give only easy unseen retrieves. If your dog has been taught early to hunt to the click he will rapidly gain confidence and his speed will increase. However, while he will hunt for a seen dummy with great perseverence, if he does not find an unseen dummy he will rapidly lose confidence and think there is nothing to find; he stops hunting and his speed and obedience suffer.

Training for unseen retrieves is dived into three parts: (1) the quick and accurate getaway; (2) the middle-distance confidence, and (3) the far distance obedience.

The quick getaway is achieved by sending the dog for unseen dummies a few yards out and when he quickly goes out to collect them, adding diversionary dummies for him to ignore.

Middle-distance confidence is established by a double dummy technique. Two or three unseen dummies are placed at forty yards out so that the dog will immediately find one or other of them as soon as he arrives in the area. Thus by quick success confidence is established.

Far-distance obedience has to be instilled into the dog and this is done by a variation of the 'three-card trick'. Set the dog upwind of a hidden dummy so that he cannot scent it and throw out first one and then another dummy at right angles to each other. Walk back about a hundred yards and signal the dog on to the unseen dummy.

Finally, send the dog for unseen dummies at first in easy situations where there is little cover, gradually extending the distance and the amount of cover until a polished performance is achieved in any conditions. It must again be emphasised that a dog will mark by the sound of the dummy falling, so all dummies should be well hidden before the lesson, throwing them the last twenty yards or so to avoid leaving a track scent. Then send the dog in from a different direction to the one you took to hide the dummy. Alternatively, if the dog's eyes are covered and the dummy thrown, at least a thump should be made behind the dog to distract his attention from the sound of the dummy falling.

It is also suggested with due deference that use be made of

markers during advanced training. It is essential that when handling a dog on to an unseen dummy the handler himself should know exactly where the dummy is. Advanced training should be varied—three or four short retrieves followed by a very long one. If the dog goes out crooked in the long retrieve, he should be stopped immediately, straightened up and then pushed out in small runs so that control is not lost. If he is allowed to get up speed in the wrong direction, it is difficult to get him on the right lines again, so 'stop—go' is the order of the day.

Advanced training, therefore, consists of (1) the establishment of the built-in obedience, (2) the speeding up of your dog and building up of his confidence, (3) teaching him perseverence, (4) teaching him to work on different grounds and in difficult conditions, and (5) allowing him to develop his style and quality.

While little variety is practised in initial training, in advanced training the handler tries to imagine every conceivable condition that he may experience in the shooting field and then watches to see how the dog performs.

Further exercises for advanced training

(1) Hide a dummy. Fire a shot in the opposite direction so that the shot and smoke hit the ground, then send the dog for the dummy. He will wish to go where he has seen the shot strike.

(2) Throw an unseen dummy near a wood or riverbank. Place the dog twenty yards from it and retire eighty yards. Click the dog to hunt. The object of the exercise is to make the dog hunt a small area without going into the wood or down the bank.

(3) Train the dog in fog or at twilight, making it difficult for you to see the dog or the dog to see you.

(4) Send the dog across the river, standing at varying distances away from the riverbank.

(5) Knock the ball with a racket into some trees so that the

dog will be out of view for short periods, then send the dog. Country for this should be carefully chosen; although you are not likely to lose your dog at this stage of training, it is still a training exercise and you should be able to see well enough from time to time to help him.

More and more birds are now introduced. Pigeons can usually be obtained from a loft and may be used in several ways. The pigeons may be put in a small hole in the ground with a slate attached to a string over the hole. As the dog approaches the hole the slate is pulled off and the pigeon takes to the air in front of the dog's nose. Alternatively, pigeons can be mesmerised by tucking their heads under their wings and then rocking them. They can then be placed on the ground and will not move for some time. The dog is led up to them and the bird is flushed.

However, the best use of a live bird is to throw it on to the dog's nose when he is not expecting it. The pigeon will either alight on the ground in front of the dog, and then take off, or will flutter in front of his nose and fly away without alighting. This is, of course, an excellent test of steadiness.

At this stage, in spite of the rabbit pen, the dog is still very interested in body scent rather than in blood scent, of which he has had little experience. During advanced training he should be given more and more opportunities to work on blood scent, so that he knows what his job really is and will grow used to retrieving live game without getting too excited.

You must now take more and more opportunities to train with professional trainers—'out to Tom's', Tom Southwerd, that is. Tom lives in Out Rawcliffe, an area of coastal Lancashire which, like the rest of the Fylde countryside, is a warren of lanes where it is impossible not to get lost. When I am finding my way through the Fylde and turn a corner, I always expect to meet my younger self of a few years ago still trying to find his way out. Last time I was going to Tom's and took a short cut and got lost as usual, I stopped to ask the way. 'Do you know of a farm near here with some white railings, belonging to Tom Southwerd?' says I.

'No,' says he, 'there be no farm with white rails hereabouts. Who did you say owned it?'

'Tom Southwerd,' says I.

'Ah,' says he, 'go about three miles from here in that direction'—pointing northwards—'that be Southwerd country. Ask anyone there and they'll know Tom Southwerd's and put you right.'

How wonderfully deep are the roots of the true countryman!

Tom's hospitality is as generous as his knowledge of dogs. Anyone who is keen on shooting and dogs is at home at Tom's. If you are a novice he will be kind to you—if you consider yourself an expert he will try you out. Tom knows a dog but will not offer advice unless asked, or unless, he knows you very well. When you do ask him, his advice is very well worth following. While you are a novice he will aid and advise you all he can: once he has decided you are proficient no fair holds are barred. But don't smile when he gets into trouble himself, as he will, because he will always find his way out—and remember you yourself will be in worse trouble very soon and will not know how to!

You should know enough now about the training of dogs to refuse retrieves that are too difficult. In the same way a too-easy retrieve is not worth the collecting. It is better to put down your dog and collect it yourself. The only time for an easy retrieve at this stage is when your dog has had a failure or is tired and uninterested. An easy retrieve may make him forget about his failure and liven him up.

We have now established a pattern: in the beginning train by yourself, then train on alternate days with a friend, finally train with as many people and dogs as you can so long as the dogs are reasonable ones. And even at this stage there is still room for a quiet session—in fact, always come back to the playing fields of Eton after a few sessions on Tom Tiddler's ground.

I was driving up to the rough shoot for advanced training when a red fox crossed the road in front of my car. Looking up, I saw a shining black horse silhouetted against an emerald green hillside. On arrival the noise of spring was almost deafening. Snipe were drumming, curlews were performing their nuptial flight, sheep and lambs in the distance were noisily asking to be fed—probably thinking I was their shepherd. The mallard and his duck got off the reed bed and plovers were running in the grass to and from their nesting places. I leaned on the gate and idly wondered whether I could train the bitch to find me plovers' eggs. This, of course, would be easy, but I decided that I could find them just as well myself by just watching the plovers running to and from their nests before taking to flight. Anyway the collecting of plovers' eggs is illegal. That day I did not feel like work, so we went for a long country walk. We strolled about and visited all our wild friends and felt quite annoyed if they were not there and engaged about their business. This probably did the dog as much good as retrieving and there were plenty of walls to get over and ditches to cross. This is the time with a trained dog when you tighten up heeling, and a walk like this makes a splendid opportunity. To improve heeling, 'hup' your dog and walk on ten yards, then pat him up with your left hand to your left side—and as he is walking at heel occasionally caress him with your left hand. It is also advisable sometimes, but not too often, to carry and swing your lead in your right hand. In these ways the dog is gradually taught to prefer being on the left side.

13 The errors of an amateur

The most usual mistake an amateur makes is to give his dog too many retrieves and retrieves beyond his capabilities. This is because he loves and is proud of his dog and wants to demonstrate him. The dog disobeys and forfeits confidence and instead of progressing steadily, loses training. It cannot be emphasised too often that a dog should never be given an exercise unsuitable to his age or state of training. In teaching a puppy to mark the dummy should not be thrown too far out or in too rough cover; in teaching a dog to hunt the same applies. A dog is not judged by what he does but by how he does it, and in the end it is only the opinion of the owner of the dog that matters and not the opinion of bystanders unless they are experienced. The expert will not take a difficult retrieve unsuitable for his dog. He will also refuse a too easy one as it will teach the dog nothing.

The amateur is always in a hurry to make progress, in other words to run before he can walk. I have seen young dogs of twelve months old being given unseen retrieves far out and in difficult cover. All amateurs wish to see their dog working in cover with live game in his mouth—neither of which is necessary or desirable until an advanced state of training.

Training is a graduated series of exercises, each one firmly implanted in a dog's mind before the next is tried with frequent refresher courses, and at the least setback an easier exercise given. I remember when I was a complete novice planting a dummy on the other side of a hedge and sending my dog for it. I was gently told that this was an advanced exercise and instructed to plant the dummy twenty yards from the dog and send him to hunt for it.

The next error the amateur makes occurs when the dog is not doing well, suddenly starts doing badly an exercise he has done well, or starts being disobedient. The amateur asks himself, 'What is wrong with my dog?' but seldom 'What am I doing wrong?'. The first thing to find out is why the dog is behaving like that. Perhaps the handler has altered his routine and confused him. It cannot be emphasised too often that all training routine must be meticulously carried out. Perhaps the handler has changed his signals and is giving some the dog is not used to and does not understand. These minor points are important in training. A friend can often see what is wrong when the trainer cannot see it for himself; but remember, when things go wrong don't just blame the dog, try to find out the reason, think it over in bed at night and then correct it, and remember it is probably you who are at fault— that stamp of the foot to make him 'Hup' when delivering the dummy may have put him off coming up to you willingly and quickly.

The amateur often loses concentration when the dog is working, perhaps engaging in conversation when the dog is out hunting for a dummy. The handler must concentrate entirely until the dummy is actually in his hand, otherwise the dog soon knows that he has lost interest and will become as slack at his work as the handler in his.

How often have I said to myself when my dog is out, 'What do I do now?' Usually if the dog has been sent out, has gone

Concentration to ensure a good delivery

No relaxation until the bird is in the hand

in the wrong direction and not been straightened up in time, it is best to recall him and start all over again. Amateurs do not like doing this. If the dog is obviously going wrong, it is best to let him settle down before using the stop whistle or giving a direction signal. I must repeat that the object of training is neither to teach disobedience, which the handler does if the dog disobeys him, nor to punish the dog for disobedience which the handler has to do when the dog disobeys. If you are uncertain what to do, it is far better to wait and see and do nothing. How many amateurs are content to do this? A typical example of knowing when not to interfere occurred at a trial, when through a mistake a dog was sent out on a marked retrieve and the judge said, 'Recall him.'. The handler did nothing and pretended not to hear. Afterwards he said, 'What was the use? I knew the dog wouldn't stop'. The amateur must learn when not to whistle.

'It is in your own time'—I have had this said to me often. The amateur wishes at all costs to collect the dummy or the bird in the shortest possible time. Usually in training this is the last thing one requires of the dog. Another dummy can always be thrown. In a trial, as long as the dog has reached the area expeditiously and is left in that area, the search for the bird is in the handler's own time. The amateur pinpoints the dummy and directs the dog on to it with much wild waving, whistling and even shouts. The professional directs the dog to the area with no excessive fuss or commands, correcting the animal only when he goes astray, and the dog, having arrived at the area, often of considerable size, is quietly allowed to demonstrate his hunting ability. After all, the game may have run or the gun may have made a mistake. Time and time again after my dog has picked a dummy from an unsuspected spot, I have said to myself, 'Well, I never thought it was there.' If this can happen with dummies, how much more often can it happen on game!

An amateur is so often absorbed in training and watching his young dog that he fails to take advantage of every opportunity of watching or criticising other dogs at work. He must develop a critical eye and learn from the mistakes of others. He must spend as much time as possible watching other dogs —how they go out, how they hunt, how they deliver—and in every case he must say to himself, 'How does my dog compare with the dog I'm watching?' If the comparison is unfavourable to his own dog, he must give him the simple exercise necessary to improve him. Later when the amateur is working against other dogs he must notice how they behave —if they are drifting downwind he must be prepared to send his dog out upwind of the dummy so as to correct the fault.

Once a professional handler came up to me after disaster had overtaken me on a trial—'Well,' he said, 'are you satisfied with your dog?' I said, 'I suppose he has not done too badly.' The professional said, 'You should be satisfied, you know,' then turned on his heel and left me. It was great encouragement and I have remembered it ever since with gratitude. The amateur must, then, assiduously practise looking at and silently criticising other dogs until some day someone will say of him, 'He knows a dog.'

It is very easy to overtrain your dog and the amateur often falls into this error. The dog becomes stale and slovenly—he is not capable either of learning new lessons or of performing properly the ones he has learnt. Another form of overtraining is by making the dog too dependent on his master, and a third way is by taking him to too many shoots without sufficient interval. His performance will deteriorate. A dog is seldom bored by dummy work, but occasionally he is if he has had a lot of the real thing. In this case he is still trained on dummies but is given very few retrieves—let him watch other dogs working in front of him to make him jealous. A dog who is lackadaisical should only be given a couple of retrieves and then returned to his kennel.

Amateurs tend to get over-excited and this reacts upon their dogs. Some dogs at the beginning of the day are very worked up but settle as the day goes on, and in the afternoon both the handler and his dog are doing much better work; other dogs seem to get worse and worse as the day goes on. The handler should try to correct his dog's mood both when he is training and when he is with him away from the training ground, and at the same time to control his own excitement. While allowing the dog to enjoy himself he should quell symptoms of over-excitement by making him settle a few yards away from him; if the dog is put down at the handler's feet he will persist in demanding attention.

The amateur often wishes to try out his dog on a runner at a very early stage in his development and, having done so, then wishes to practise the retrieving of runners because this gives him great kudos and, he thinks, trains his dog. In fact the exact opposite is the case! A dog who has been well trained to hunt will automatically learn to puzzle out the scent of a runner and the finding of runners will come naturally to him. However, if he is trained on them at too early an age, he will not only be made excitable but may even become hard-mouthed or so keen on following the runner that he could neglect a dead bird for the more exciting chase. It cannot be emphasised too often that the handler's job is to teach his dog to hunt an area systematically, and to keep his dog steady , and not to encourage him to dash off into the blue. Neither amateurs nor dogs must go mad on runners.

I have described some of the general errors of the amateur. Having made a mistake, you say to yourself, 'I'll never make that mistake again.' Unfortunately, of course, you do—the circumstances are a little different and you forget your previous mistake. However, if you really learn to watch your dog, mistakes will not occur so often: watch to see if his tail is wagging when he is on a scent; watch to see if his attention is on you when he is 'hupped' or whether he is looking round; watch to see if he has settled down or is still excited; watch to see how he is hunting—and if he takes a line, whether he really means it or not. In this way your dog should be able to tell you what is happening, and by following his lead you will be able to help him and not hinder him.

14 The first and second seasons

The first season—'Ware hares'

When you arrive at the meeting place, let your dog run about a bit and get used to the cars, the other strange dogs and the men, but keep a wary eye open that he does not get into trouble. It is rather a strange fact, but dogs out for a shooting day and ready to work together rarely quarrel or snap, so let your dog mill around with the rest until he has settled down, then put him back into the car or call him to heel if you are ready to move off.

It is extremely difficult both to shoot and train. The first thing to note is that we try to make our dog as inconspicuous as possible, keeping him on a tight lead in the shooting brake and not letting him off the lead until we are actually at our stands or walking over the stubble. In fact, a good saying to remember is that when the other guns have their dogs off the lead, you should have your dog on it, and when the guns have their dogs pegged down at the covert side, yours should be sitting beside you free.

A long retrieve

The next thing to remember is that it is useless to let your dog pick easy retrieves lying in full sight. The dog may get only one or possibly two retrieves a day. The rest are not worth while sending him for, so should be picked by hand, as he will learn nothing from such retrieves and hand-picking promotes steadiness. Again, the dog has to take precedence over the shooting, so before you raise your gun, look down to see that your dog is steady and 'hup' him if necessary. It is better not to fire at a bird rather than let your dog run in even once, since if he does he will have to be punished and disciplined, and training may be held up for weeks. It is almost impossible to punish a dog correctly on a shooting day.

The dog should only be allowed to collect at most two hares during his first season. This is to establish that he has

Bringing back an unsighted retrieve

learned to carry them properly, turning them over, picking them up by the back to that they are equally balanced at both sides of his mouth. Training for carrying hares can be accomplished by filling a large dummy with loose sand so that it sags on either side when the dog picks it up in the middle. As hares are the big bugbear of any shooting dog, the dog must be firmly taught to leave them alone so that he is really steady to them. If you are unfortunate enough to be involved in a hare drive with many hares coming slowly towards you, the best thing to do is to put your dog on a lead; then you know he cannot run in.

Certain types of game like snipe are distasteful to dogs. This fault is easily surmounted. If the dog refuses a snipe, pick it up, put it in your pocket until it has got your smell on it, and then throw it a few yards and encourage the dog to fetch it. It is always a good plan on a shooting day to ask the keeper if you can pocket the first partridge shot; then if your dog fails on a retrieve the partridge can be quickly dropped for the dog to pick.

One of the troubles the amateur handler encounters is that the other dogs are seldom steady, and there is nothing worse for your dog than to send him out and have other dogs appear from nowhere. The only thing to be done is to 'hup' your dog and bring him in to you, and then drop the partridge that you have secreted and send him quietly out on his own for it.

If a gun says that a bird is down, make quite sure in your own mind that he has spoken the truth before you send your dog. If you know the gun, it is an easy decision to make, but don't let your dog hunt endlessly for a bird that is not there. Remember again: no failures! And the bird in the pocket that can be dropped! Another thing, don't send your dog after an old cock who is a very strong runner in case he gets scratched and you make the dog inclined to nip the bird. In fact, your dog should be tried on very few runners during his first season. However, it is a proud moment when there is a difficult retrieve and the captain of the shoot asks you to send your dog to collect it.

The best kind of shooting day for the first season is for you and a couple of friends to go out on to a rough shoot where you can spend your time at retrieving game undisturbed and the shooting will be secondary.

Grouse-shooting comes into a different category, and there is nothing better than to take your own dog on a day's grouse-shooting, provided he is kept well in the butt whilst the grouse are going over and the lead is put on if he shows the least sign of unsteadiness.

You may be offered a few picking-up days. This is not entirely a blessing unless you use it as such, as there are far too many retrieves to do, most of them too easy. A dog is not improved by this. A few retrieves well done with the dog under control is what you are aiming for. If you do go on a picking-up day, it is as well to stand well back from the guns so as to pick the birds that have been shot and carried on.

Another difficulty is that one of the guns, knowing you have a highly trained dog, may ask you to retrieve a bird which you do not think is within the capacity of your dog. You must be prepared to refuse gracefully and suggest that the retrieve be made by the keeper's dog.

Pigeon-shooting is ideal for teaching a young dog. He has to exercise patience, the retrieves can be made as easy or as difficult as required, and the handler can take as much time as he wants with no audience to watch him. However it is of course essential that the handler learns to work not only in front of other handlers who know the difficulties but also in front of other shooting men who do not fully appreciate what is happening. If a criticism is made of you and your dog, the first thing you say to yourself is: who has done the criticising?

The shooting man talks endlessly and authoritatively about dogs and considers himself a good judge. It is unfortunate that in so many cases his dogs are so ill-behaved. This is because the dog to him is of secondary importance to his shooting and he does not take the trouble to understand him. He sends his dog to be trained and then is quite astonished when, without waiting for his dog to transfer his allegiance, he cannot manage it in the field. He blames the trainer. His ideas of punishment are also elementary; if the dog goes wrong, give it a beating. The old keeper, however, who suggested that the guns should give their dogs a beating before proceeding to the first covert was at least trying to keep his game undisturbed! The keeper's dog is a handy animal, usually well disciplined, and knows how to hunt. Normally, however, he is not self-reliant and works only near his master. He has been well named 'the keeper's stooge'. The keeper returns the compliment by referring to the field trial dogs as 'those circus animals'.

At the end of the day the guns return to the shooting hut and, after discussing the bag, usually go on to dogs and sex. It is unfortunate that they know so little about dogs!

The shooting man says that he doesn't wish to direct his dog—he can always walk over and then let his dog hunt, or alternatively he wants to go on a rough shoot so lets his dog hunt in front of him. These are valid arguments, and many a rough shooting dog gives excellent service to his master. However, all gundogs if they are to be of real use in the field require disciplining, handling, and occasional refresher courses. Then, after three years, if you do not wish to go in for trials, you can let your dog hunt in front of you. As to handling, there are runners with other birds down, dykes you can't cross and pheasants that are difficult to find. All handling is discipline and without discipline the dog is more nuisance than he is worth. Often one has seen a gun's shooting day spoilt because of his dog, not to mention the other guns. I cannot agree that shooting should be the beginning and end of your enjoyment, and anybody who enjoys the countryside and shooting should be able to watch and enjoy a good dog working, just as he is prepared to watch and enjoy the work of the beaters.

A final warning: handle your dog as if you were training him for trials. Eye him before you shoot. If you are going to send him on a retrieve, take the cartridges out of your gun, lay the gun on the ground, take the whistle out of your pocket and 'set' your dog, and then with due ceremony send him to find the game.

The second season—'No lending of leads'

'Greater trust hath no man than he who lends his lead to his friend.'

Your dog is now fully trained and should be obedient and steady. However, a dog takes time to settle down and become completely trustworthy. Finally he becomes your constant friend, helper and companion, but on no account must he be allowed to take advantage of his master even when he is completely adult. So nurse him along and take the same trouble with him as you did in his first season. He may now be

Retrieving hare: well balanced, correctly held by the back and well up

allowed to practise on runners, but be wary of hares.

During the second season your shooting will no doubt improve. After glancing at the dog you will now take the shot with calm deliberation. You will be asked to collect more and more difficult retrieves, but you can still say 'leave it to the keeper's dog'. It must be stressed that it is easy even at this stage to ruin an animal. The ordinary shot never seems to realise this, or if he does will not take the trouble to make his shooting a secondary to the training of his dog.

A question often asked is how much you should take your dog out shooting. The answer depends upon the dog. As long as he does not deteriorate and grow wilful, he should be taken out as often as you can. However, if he has a single bad day when he misbehaves, you should stop taking him out and start re-training him on the training grounds until discipline has been re-established.

I consider that hares are animals of the chase and not of the shooting field. Coursing of hares is the natural way of hunting them, with a quick death by the greyhound breaking the hare's back. The handler of a retriever must never let his dog pick a wounded hare. It might get up and run, and then the dog's training could be put back three or four months if he gives chase.

From the moment you slip the lead on your dog, training has ceased as temptation no longer exists. However, it is better to put the lead on than to let him run in. In the first season he is better on a lead during a hare drive, although it is quite possible that his behaviour will be better in the first season than in the second!

In the second season leave him off the lead but remember that the hare drive is the worst temptation of all to a dog. Concentrate on your dog and only shoot a hare if your dog is steady, otherwise allow them to pass you in the hope that your host will not notice this aberration. However, you have also got a duty to your host. If he wants the hares shot, as no doubt he will, as he has the farmers to consider, slip the dog on a lead, relax and shoot the hares.

In dog training there is only one person of importance and that is the dog; so if your dog misbehaves in the morning of a formal shoot, leave him in the car in the afternoon.

The successful working of a dog, like any other sport, needs in the end the killer instinct, but you will never succeed if you use this instinct against your dog—you must use it only when things go against you in the field, to give him that extra bit of confidence or authority which he may need.

'They are all illegitimate'

15 On judges and judging

The *Guide to Field Trial Judges* (Appendix 2) and *Kennel Club Field Trial Rules* (extracts in Appendix 3) may be obtained from the Kennel Club, and all handlers should have read and digested them. It is emphasised that the following rules apply only to retriever trials.
Judges may be on either Panel 'A' or Panel 'B' or invited to judge prior to being proposed to the 'B' list.
Panel 'A' judges must have judged two open and two other stakes held by different societies.
Panel 'B' is by recommendation, but the judge must have judged at least one stake—panel 'A' Judges are promoted by the Kennel Club from the 'B' list, when they have had sufficient experience (Field Trial Regulation No. 5).
Championship stakes—all 'A' judges.
Open and all-age stakes—two 'A' judges.
Non-winner and other stakes—one 'A' judge.
Often there are three judges to a stake. When there are four judges they must judge in pairs.

No dog is discarded until he has run under two judges, unless he has committed a major crime. Crimes are assessed as follows:

Eliminating faults: hard-mouth, whining or barking, running in, chasing, out of control, failure to enter water.

Major faults: failure to find game, unsteadiness at heel, eyewipe, disturbing ground, slack and unbusinesslike work, noisy handling, poor control, changing birds.

Credit points: natural game-finding ability, nose, marking ability, drive and style, quickness in finding game, control, quietness in handling, retrieving and delivery.

But no dog shall be allowed to do anything in a trial which in the opinion of the judges might not prove to be useful work in an ordinary day's shooting.

Diplomas and certificates of merit are given at the discretion of the judges. When a bird is shot very close to the dog, the judge should offer it to another judge. Judges should see that their dog gets its chance in the correct order, starting with the lowest number on the right, but if the second or subsequent dogs are successful on a retrieve, this dog has the chance of the next retrieve. A dog should have a minimum of two retrieves before the next dog is called up. Judges should give full credit for marking. Judges should not penalise a dog for putting the game down so as to get a better grip.

At some working tests judges use a system of points. There is nothing wrong in this and it may give a lead to the best dog, always provided that the judge can use his own discretion when the points have been summed up—and give bonus marks for good dogs and minus marks for dogs which, although they have performed their tasks, are lacking in that essential quality and brilliance required in a first-class dog.

It has been known for a judge at a field trial to use a stop watch. This is fantastic and shows a complete lack of the qualities required of a judge. A retrieve should be judged by its quality and not by its speed. A very poor dog may stumble on the game and make good time, yet command few marks. In a working test, however, which is more of a competition, it would be allowable to use a stop watch so long as the retrieve is a seen one and the dummies are placed in exactly the same place and there are obstacles to surmount, preferably water.

At the Games Fair the judges use a points system and the number of points allotted to each dog is announced at the end of each run. This allows the spectators to do their own judging and see how near their opinion was to that of the judge. Thus, there is possibly a use for the points system in working tests, but I think that in major trials it is best to have three or four judges backing their own opinions and reaching a decision among themselves.

Judges are advised in open stakes to ask their guns not to shoot directly over a dog when it is out working. In puppy, novice and non-winner stakes, judges should advise their guns not to shoot at all while the dogs are out working. All eyewipes should be treated on their merits, that is to say if the first dog never reaches the area and the next dog is sent out and collects the game, the second dog should not be credited with an eye-wipe. However, if a dog has thoroughly searched the area and failed to find the bird, the handler of the next dog down, if he can take advantage of the last dog's mistakes, will not only be credited by the judge with an eye-wipe but can also help his dog to success. The bird, of course, may have run in an unexpected direction or the wind may be wrong. This is where a good handler may step in provided he has summed up the situation correctly.

The area

In field trials, if a handler gets his dog into the area, the judge will not only give him time to find the game but during this time the judge will be able to assess how the dog works and the handler may be building up points in his own favour.

The judge does not want a circus dog with the handler blowing and waving and finally putting the dog on a sixpence. This only restricts the dog's natural style and ability.

It is easy for a handler to visualise the area at thirty to forty yards when the contour of the ground can be seen, but not so easy to visualise it at one hundred yards. At this range more licence must be given to your dog, but it must be remembered that the judge probably has the same difficulty as the handler.

The field trial judge has only one duty, that is to assess the work of a dog on a specific date. One might say that this is all a show judge has to do, but standards of beauty are somewhat variable and it is often thought, probably erroneously, that a show judge is swayed possibly by a dog's pedigree and the pedigree of the man or woman at the other end of the string. In a field trial, if a dog commits a basic crime such as running in, he is put out of the trial, and this is obvious for all to see. At one trial I was at, nine dogs were put out before lunchtime and this must have helped the judges considerably in their final choice.

In the case of hard-mouth, as all birds have to be handed to the judge after delivery and runners are handed over alive, it avails one naught to pretend to kill a dead bird. If the judge thinks a dog has hard-mouth—a major crime—he must show the bird to the other judges and the handler before he can put a dog out of the trial, as sometimes a bird is damaged by the fall. It is therefore quite correct, if there is any doubt, to keep a dog in the trial, but he is suspect and any bird he picks after this must be closely examined by his judge. If another bird is damaged, the dog must be put out at once. Similarly, if an apparently unshot bird is picked by one of the dogs, this also has to be examined by at least one other of the three judges in case it is a pricked bird and has the blood scent on it.

The object of a retriever is, of course, to retrieve game, so that, provided he retrieves, the dog should be carried on through the stake however poor his work is: given an adequate amount of game. However, if a dog has a failure it is extremely unlikely that he will get any further except in a puppy or non-winners' stake, unless the bird is never picked when, of course, it does not count against him. If the dog before you has failed to pick a bird and you are next to be called in to retrieve it, you will be given the next retrieve following it.

Many handlers complain of the time the judge allows them for picking the bird. This in most cases is grossly unfair to the judge. The handler's duty is to get his dog into the area as expeditiously as possible, then allow the dog to hunt but keep him in the area. Once the dog is in the area the handler is working in his own time and the judge will give him endless latitude.

Once I was told to call my dog in after only a minute or two. The pheasant had fallen about fifty yards out in a field of rough grass over a hedge. I sent the dog through the hedge, but it was quite obvious that I could not push him out on to the field beyond as he was hunting the hedge—quite obvious, I must say, both to myself and the judge, so he immediately and rightly told me to call my dog in.

The handler and the dog come under at least two of the judges in the course of a trial and the winners are decided between the judges. A judge, therefore, marks as follows: he first gives a retrieve or a failure to each dog for the actual retrieve and then he marks on style, marking ability, handling, obedience to orders, and delivery. If a dog gets a very easy retrieve the judge will give him a success but obviously cannot mark him up as he has not had an opportunity to show his quality. Sometimes you have an exceptionally good dog not winning in a field trial because he has not had the opportunity of showing his worth.

The judges are always very human and endeavour to help the handler as much as possible. After all, it is the dog who is being judged and not the handler. The judge will often tell you if you are hunting your dog in the wrong area, and on occasion a judge has told me not to whistle my dog but to let him hunt. Once a judge apologised to me for sending my young dog out to a hare which was only wounded when the judge thought it dead. All handlers should remember that this is a sport for the enjoyment of all, and if they cannot accept their reverses with a smile they should not be in the field. We all get plenty of reverses at trials. One day the opportunity will come your way and if a dog has been properly trained you will be able to take advantage of it.

On being asked to judge

It may occur to the amateur that he will never be asked to judge a trial but, provided he has trained a dog and has successfully run it—and has studied the *Guide to Field Trial Judges* (Appendix 2)—there is no reason why he should not act as a judge under more experienced judges. This, of course, is a mixed blessing. It is very hard work which carries a lot of responsibility, and the rewards are few. However, if the amateur decides to take the plunge and he is asked, he should first find out who are his fellow judges so that the trial may be run in harmony and peace.

The embryo judge should have clearly defined views on how to decide between the dogs running. Copious notes are not necessary and are even confusing. He is given a book marked from 1—24 in a two-day stake, and from now on the dogs are known by their numbers. He then uses the judges' shorthand—R for retrieve, F for fail, to which is added PH—Pheasant, SN—Snipe, R—rabbit, to denote what the dog has retrieved. He also notes the type of ground, and he can add 'runner' next. The judge puts EW—1, 2 or 3 denoting if it was an eye wipe, whether the dog succeeded first, second or third down. Then he can add P.D. (poor delivery), heel ?, mouth ?, M ? (marking), control ?, and finally he ends his shorthand with VG, G, F, P—to denote whether the general work of the dog was very good or poor. From this he can grade them into A, B and C categories. These brief notes recall to the judge's memory the actual retrieve and also allows him to compare the dog's performance with that of the other dogs. After the trial the judge should destroy his notes.

It must be remembered that there are no additions and subtractions in field trials. If a dog fails, he is out—but any dog who survives the first day should have a chance of winning on the second, when it is possible he may put up one or two 'spectaculars'. It is possible, and occurs, that a superb dog who is carried on may only achieve a certificate because he has had no opportunity of showing his worth, and many a good dog has been eye-wiped at a trial by a poor dog and the experienced handler knows that a poor dog will not last the course.

At various times during the trial, the judges meet and decide what dogs to discard, until finally there are about five dogs left in for the run-off, and these dogs are run off under the eyes of all the judges—both the dogs and the judges being in the centre of the line. At this time the judges have complete discretion as to which dog they send off for any given retrieve.

At the end of the trial, a novice handler who is in doubt may approach a judge and ask his opinion of the dog: the judge will be very helpful and proffer good advice. If you are a novice judge it is advisable to refer the handler to a senior judge.

The judges' steward obtains your two dogs from the dog steward and keeps a check on the dogs you have had under you, the lower number being on the right. When the right-hand dog has had his two tries, you call for another dog and the left-hand dog then moves over to your right. It is most important that you remember that your right hand dog has the next retrieve.

It is, of course, the judge's duty to help the handler in marking to the best of his ability, but it is in the end the handler's responsibility how and where he 'handles' his dog. So, to the handlers I say, 'Don't criticise the judge—he is trying his best. Perhaps it is you who are at fault'.

16 Of guns, stewards and professional trainers

It might not be amiss to mention the guns and stewards, without whom trials could not take place.

The guns have a trying task—shooting before a large gallery with long waits in between while dogs are sent to retrieve. They are mostly walking up and shooting 'going away' birds with instructions to let the birds get a reasonable distance away before shooting them. They also know that the handler wants a dead bird and that if the gun misses, not only are the judge and the handler disappointed but there may not be enough birds to complete the trial reasonably early. Field trial people are always deeply grateful to the owner of the shoot and to the guns who turn out to shoot on the day. I have only one suggestion to make to them—don't talk to the handlers and keep a reasonable distance away from them.

On the question whether another bird should be shot when one is down, this depends on the trial—non-winner stakes or open stakes—and the judge usually gives directions to the guns about it. However, most handlers will be grateful if the

GUNS, STEWARDS AND PROFESSIONAL TRAINERS 143

gun does shoot, if they see that the bird drops a reasonable distance from the dog.

Stewarding is a rewarding occupation to the novice. He has a front-line view, is in close contact with the judge and can learn from the judge's opinions. Occasionally a steward has made a remark which the handler thought the judge had made and acted accordingly. To the stewards I would suggest: speak as little as possible and do not be too officious. The handler already has enough problems to contend with.

On professional handlers:—In the field trial world it is considered bad form to talk of your dogs. This, of course, is for two reasons—the first that any professional can judge in a trice what a dog is worth—'A good wine needs no bush'—and secondly because a glowing account of your dog's excellence may bolster up your own morale but is exceedingly boring to the listener, who is probably itching to inflict the same torture on you. This kind of conversation is the sign of an amateur. Being an amateur myself I will try to avoid it! However, I will mention three of my own dogs, each of completely different temperament.

There was Judy, of undistinguished pedigree who somewhere in her ancestry must have had quality blood, a plodder but steady and natural worker who knew far more about the game than I did.

Then there was the big-balled bouncer, named for obvious anatomical reasons, who lived up to his name in thought, word and deed, was sometimes brilliant but did not rise to the big occasion, when something always seemed to go snap in his brain and no amount of training or punishment could alter the fact. He had a regrettable tail which made him so easily recognised in the field that none of his mistakes could be covered up, and he was allowed to sink into oblivion. It is a fact that all my dogs seem to have regrettable tails of some sort or another but the bouncer's topped the lot, as it curled generously over his back.

Then there was Susan, who dropped at a sneeze and who could never be punished, whose confidence had to be built up step by step and who was easily put off by a gruff voice. She had to be given endless affection and licence to try to make her self-reliant. I have seen her often confused but never wilful, self-willed or obstinate.

These and other dogs one has known only underline the fact that all dogs have to be trained differently according to their individual character.

Provided you are not given to boasting about your dog's prowess, professionals are the kindest people in the world and go to endless trouble to help you and put your dog on the right lines, and they go out of their way to praise any good retrieve your dog has made. Among themselves they are perhaps a little more outspoken, as the professional who said to a friend of his when they were watching a dog perform at a trial: 'You know, I really don't believe that dog could find a covey of tramcars,' or on the other occasion when the dog was trying hard but the handler was confusing the dog: 'You know,' the professional said, 'I don't think that handler knows which end to put in the biscuit.'

Finally there is the story of the handler who was extolling his dog and said, 'You know, my dog has a nose like a vacuum cleaner!'—'With the fuse burnt out,' was the retort!

The professional will help you all he can but he is human after all. He knows his ground and he knows the way of dogs. That easy-looking retrieve he has set you may not be so easy after all. Do not go out in expert company until the basic training has been completed. Let's face it, even the professional doesn't suffer fools gladly—so try to listen and not bore him, and remember that he will never proffer advice unless you ask for it. Then he will give it and it will be well worth listening to.

'If at first you don't succeed . . .'

17 Working tests and field trials

Working tests are in many ways more relaxed affairs than field trials and are excellent for trying out the dog, and the element of luck is eliminated as each dog has similar retrieves. Usually the first retrieve is a moderately long, seen one with a diversion dummy thrown to the side or rear. The second is a seen retrieve over a wire fence. The third should be a long seen water retrieve in which the handler should not speak to his dog. Possibly there is a long marked retrieve on land where again the handler should not speak. They may also give you a fairly long unseen retrieve. There is no chance of runners, and dummies are easy to mark, all falling at about the same spot, so the handler has a relatively easy time of it. Finally, of course, there is the run-off.

Working tests are run on the same lines as field trials but the conditions are not quite so severe—after all they are tests, not trials. In fact, they are competitions. Working tests are an excellent test of how the dog has been trained and handled. They are not a good test of the reaction of the dog under stress. Dummies do not compensate for live game and there can be no surprises in working tests. However much one tries to the contrary, they are still artificial and not the real thing. They are, in fact, a training ground. The amount of work put into the tests by the organisers must be appreciable. It is not easy to lay out seen and unseen retrieves for sixteen dogs and to plan five or six retrieves of gradually increasing severity. The organisers will probably be out the day previously trying their own dogs on the tests which they have set you.

Working tests, novice trials and open trials are all very different affairs. As I have explained, a working test can be considered as a competition to ascertain who has done his homework best. There is little test of a dog's steadiness and as the dogs are brought up one by one there is little testing of the dog's real ability. The handler knows exactly where the dummy lies and knows that it won't run, so even he has an easier time.

A novice trial, however, is the real thing, but as it is only for novice dogs a considerable amount of latitude is allowed. Some of the novice handlers are often very noisy and signalling wildly, and the dogs may not be taking much notice. This excess of energy on the handlers' part does not fool the judges, who are usually tolerant.

An open stake is another matter altogether. If the dog or the handler makes a mistake, he is out. To handle a dog in an open stake, the following advice is given: don't worry too much about the dog keeping strictly to heel—if the handler is always slapping his pocket and calling the dog in he will work up both himself and the dog and also be penalised. The dog should, after all, be a reasonable heeler by this time. When the game gets up and is shot the handler has three things to do in a split second (1) keep the dog steady, (2) mark the game, (3) try to decide whether it is a runner or not. Priorities must be considered here: (1) the dog must be kept steady—so look at him first (2) the dog is probably a better marker than his handler, so the marking can be left to the dog, (3) determine whether the bird is a runner or not—this is of great importance and only comes by experience. However, the judge or the gun may be asked their opinion.

When the dog is out on an unmarked bird he should be allowed to hunt a little to let off steam, so that he is sure to obey the signals when they are given him. He should be permitted a fairly large area. This is where teaching the dog to hunt in a circle to the click pays off, and if he takes a decisive line he should be allowed to follow it. Knowing your dog and trusting him comes in here. It is for you to determine whether he means business and is on a runner or is just wandering off, perhaps following a hare track. If he is on a runner and you stop him, he will not take that line again.

The rules of a field trial are very simple and as long as the handler practises the ordinary good manners of the shooting field, everyone is very helpful and pleasant. Here is a composite account of a field trial as seen by the handler.

Having filled in his form and received his acceptance and allotted number, the handler usually starts off for a trial the night before as it may be far away. He should book in at the headquarters hotel because there he is sure to meet other handlers. After he has gone a few miles on his way the handler probably checks off in his mind that he has everything he needs. Suddenly, as everything is so quiet in the back, he says to himself, 'My god, I suppose I have put the dog in the car and not left it behind?' Having reassured himself on this essential point, he proceeds on his way and starts to enjoy the journey and watch the view. In one case the trial was in Scotland. On the way up a white hare was seen, startling against the brown hillside. The change of colour of the hare in winter is for camouflage, but there is a second and possibly very important reason—as the pigment is removed from the hairs it is replaced by air bubbles, thus the hare's fur becomes a much more effective insulation against the cold of the winter —'the air in the hair of the white hare acts like a string vest'— a wonderful example of nature achieving two objects by one biological change. Incidentally, a hare's eyes are on the side of its head and tend to act independently. Thus, if a hare is being chased, he looks backwards with one eye and this causes him to run in a circle, a manoeuvre which is a blessing to many members of the footsore beagling fraternity! A hare when pursued and running straight will be able to look behind him, and if the shooter in front does not move, the hare will run right up to his feet and possibly into him.

Having arrived at his hotel, the handler may find that it is undesirable to leave his dog in the car for the night as perhaps there is no suitable garage available, or it may be terribly cold, so he approaches the night porter for permission for the dog to sleep in his room. This being granted, he orders an early breakfast and arranges for a pint of milk and a raw egg to be supplied for his dog in the morning. He also finds out the exact spot where the trial is going to be held. He then has dinner and goes to bed. Unfortunately, the dog becomes restless and starts pacing, so, fearing he will have a neurotic dog on his hands in the morning, he allows the animal to sleep on his bed, only to discover that the dog takes up all the bed and his master spends the rest of the cold and restless night wondering whether he is going to land on the floor and what has happened to all the bedclothes!

Bright and early next morning, and feeling like death from a sleepless night and trial nerves—and possibly the alcohol he had the night before—the handler gets up, breakfasts his dog, has his own breakfast and sets out for the trial.

Arriving at a good field, he gets out of the car, and after the dog has had a run round, gives him a retrieve or two, usually to find that the dog is doing everything wrong in a most uninterested manner; the handler wonders why he has ever brought to a trial an animal that has obviously never had a day's training in its life. He arrives at the meeting place and, after saying 'good morning' to one or two people he knows, takes his dog out of the car. The dog immediately shows his manhood by starting to dig himself into Australia, scattering dirt on several people standing by. The handler then takes him for a walk in a nearby field. Every other dog is behaving and looks calm and collected. The handler's dog alone is showing to his discerning eye every sign of field trial nerves and temperament—he refuses to walk quietly to heel and, coming up against a fence, decides against jumping it when told to do so. Not wishing to create a fuss or lift the dog over the fence, the handler then finds a way to get round it and joins the rest of the trial, who are now moving off.

Being No. 12, the handler will not be required at first, as only the first six numbers go into the line at the start, and for the next hour or two he watches the sport, usually thinking what easy retrieves the others are getting. His own dog is, however, getting more and more on his toes. Eventually he is called into the line. Very slowly, very steadily, he walks along the line to calm both himself and the dog until he arrives at the judge, to whom he reports, and he is given his position. The handler keeps the lead on the dog until the very last moment, indeed until he is actually told to remove it by the judge on moving off—an elementary precaution in case any thing gets up. Once the line has moved off he calls his dog to heel and concentrates on the dog. Talking to stewards and guns is to be deprecated. The handler also tries to arrange that he is never too near the guns or a steward. It is important that the handler know where the wind is coming from—if it is not obvious, a puff at a cigarette will immediately establish its direction.

The line moves off and immediately the dog starts to hunt at heel. The handler slaps his pocket but the dog takes no notice and he hopes the judge has not seen—vain hope! Suddenly a pheasant gets up off the dog's nose and the dog freezes. The judge turns to the handler, smiles and says, 'You know, he knew it was there all the time.' The handler relaxes and the line proceeds, this time the dog nicely to heel. He is hoping his first retrieve will be an easy one. However, a pheasant falls in the wood and the judge takes him forward and says, 'Your idea is as good as mine—will you please try from here.' Now is the chance to show dog handling. The dog is cast forward and clicked to hunt. He covers the ground well and is working nicely in a circle but is going too much to the right, so he is 'hupped' and brought in. The handler makes a half turn and sends the dog out more to the left but with the same result, so he is brought in again, and the judge says, 'Try more to the left again, please.' So for the third time the dog is sent out. This time with no trouble at all he picks the pheasant and makes a beautiful delivery. The gun murmurs, 'Congratulations,' and says, 'that ought to give you some marks,' and the steward smiles.

The line is rejoined and proceeds forward. An easy bird falls down the line and the judge of that section calls to the handler's judge, 'I don't want it. Do you?' The judge accepts and sends his other handler to collect it, which he does with ease. The next retrieve the handler is given some half hour later looks easy. The pheasant has fallen in a ditch fifty yards out. The dog has obviously marked it, and when the judge tells the handler he can send him out, he goes out with a rush. Ten yards from the ditch he puts on his brakes and starts questing along the ditch, going downwind. The handler lets the dog go fifty yards and then wonders if he should stop him. However, he decides it is probably a runner and not a hare track he is on. The dog disappears from view and after a few minutes the judge says, 'When did you see your dog last?'. When the handler replies, he says, 'You had better come forward with me.' They both inspect the place where the pheasant has fallen. It was obviously a runner—there are only feathers there. A deathly hush reigns and there is no sign of the dog. The judge says, 'Well, we can only wait,' and then, with a smile, 'it happened to me once, too'. Just then the dog appears with the pheasant in his mouth—again success! The judge tells the handler to put the dog on the lead and he retires to the spectators.

Soon lunch is called and the handler decides he has had a wonderful morning and must be well up among the leaders.

After lunch, with another judge the handler wipes somebody's eye over an easy retrieve—he could not control his dog, which hunted wildly and didn't stumble on the pheasant—following which the handler has to send his dog out over a

Field Trial Ch. Avenham Dictator in action (*C. M. Cooke*)

wide ditch. This entails some shouting on his part and recasting the dog twice, but he makes it and the dog collects the bird. But then comes disaster—the handler is at a stand alongside a wood and the pheasants are falling rapidly. The dog is excited. One pheasant crashes down through the trees fluttering. It is too much for the dog and the handler does not hiss at him in time to settle him. He runs in. The handler slips on his lead and says to him 'That's your lot, my son,' and to the judge, 'He's been working up to that for a long time.' The judge smiles and says, 'I know.' The handler wanders disconsolately towards the spectators—five of them are in a little bunch. They greet him with, 'Join the running-in club.' He proceeds to watch the run-off and then drive home. This is field trials. He says to himself, 'I'll never enter for one again,' but he always does.

One day your little dog will win and the other competitors

will come up to shake your hand and congratulate you. You will not only have the dog but you will have handled well, and you will be able to step in on a difficult retrieve where others have failed, and prove to the judge that your dog is good. You need all this in field trials—skill, luck and the right dog. Amateurs look at all the dogs running and say, 'He is better than mine,' or 'How can I compete against this or that professional?' Nowadays I take no notice of anything but my own dog—if he has pleased me I go home satisfied whether he has won or not.

It is not easy to run a brilliant dog in a trial. A professional's dog always looks as if it is going to run in and never does. Anyone can run a pedestrian animal and perhaps even win one trial with it, but the better your dog the more it depends on you—nay, not to fuss your dog but to step in at the critical moment. The handler needs confidence, intelligence, knowledge and humility: which are exactly the same attributes required in the dog.

Field trials from the host's point of view

There are many arrangements which a host has to think of when he is approached by the chairman of a Field Trial Society and asked if he will permit a trial to be held on his ground. If he accepts, the secretary and chairman will call to see him, and after a convenient date has been fixed they will inspect the ground with the host and his head keeper.

The first thing to arrange is the car park, because in a twenty four dog stake with competitors, spectators, guns, beaters and officials, there may be as many as fifty cars present. The Field Trial Secretary will arrange the signposting of the roads to the car park.

The Society will also arrange for the payment of the beaters and will suitably remunerate the head keeper with a good tip.

The trial is planned so that it begins by walking up on the boundaries, endeavouring to push the birds into roots or rough cover—whence they are walked up—and by walking in a circle it is hoped that by the end of the morning the trial has arrived back as near the cars as possible so that there is not a long distance to go to lunch.

Lunch is generally left if possible in a twelve dog stake until all the dogs have been under two judges.

The trial is also planned to include, if available, a water test, and should also have a formal covert shoot towards the end of the day to test dogs for steadiness and whining, otherwise covert shoots are not very useful in field trials. Too many birds are dropped either in plain view or marked by more than one gun, so that at the end of the pick-up the dogs are hunting for the birds already retrieved.

If a pond is shot over, sticks should be placed for the guns and they should shoot with their backs to the pond, in order if possible to drop their birds over a hedge and not in full sight of the dogs.

The requisite bag for a twelve-dog stake is from forty-five to sixty-five head and in a twenty-four dog two-day stake, fifty head of game on the first day and thirty on the second. As more ground is necessary in a two-day stake, it may be advisable to run the trial on adjoining estates by arrangement between the two hosts.

The host has to arrange and instruct his guns—six is the usual number of guns and six dogs in the line—two dogs and two guns to each judge, in the three judge system. They should be asked to try to shoot the birds so as to give reasonable retrieves for the dogs. In a novice stake they may be asked not to shoot when a dog is out, and in an open stake not to shoot over a dog who is working. They should also be instructed to forget their usual shooting manners, and to see that birds are killed and put on the ground. It is, therefore, perfectly correct for two guns to shoot at the same bird.

Once a trial has been arranged, the host should leave its management to his keeper. He has no responsibility for the running of the trial but should be at liberty to shoot or to talk to his friends. At the end of the trial, the host or his wife presents the cups, and after the awards are made a vote of thanks is proposed. The host replies to this, after which the winner proposes a vote of thanks to the judges and the senior judge replies.

The head keeper should be in the middle of the line and should see that the line moves forward at about half the pace of an ordinary shooting day. Before the trial begins, he should have provided an official 'picker-up' who walks with the flag man. If a judge has decided to leave a bird, a beater is left close to the spot so that the official picker-up may be correctly instructed. The head keeper is also responsible for supplying the flag man and instructing him to keep the spectators in a tight group on one side of the line. The head keeper should place responsible beaters on each side of the line and see that they fully understand the plan of the trial. All beaters are expected to tap gently with their sticks but not to speak or make undue noise.

It may be necessary for the head keeper to take his beaters out on the morning that the trial starts so as to drive the birds into cover from which they may be flushed later in the day.

If these points of organisation are carried out, the trial will proceed smoothly and efficiently and add much to the enjoyment of all.

18 The final bounce

A fit dog, fully trained, should still bounce. However, discipline must still be maintained and there must be no relaxation, however beautifully the dog performs.

One last exercise for the handler must be described. A friend plants the dummy while your dog has his eyes covered and you have yours shut. Thus neither of you knows where the damned dummy lies. Then your friend speaks thus: 'The dummy lies this-a-way, or that-a-way or forrard', 'a long shot or a short shot', and with these exhortations you send out the dog and let him hunt diligently the ground so graphically described. Or your friend can cheat a little and say the dummy lies at twenty-five yards from yon high oak when he knows full well that it lies at least fifty yards distant. Thus you learn systematically to hunt a wide area and likewise acquire a certain scepticism of any instructions given to you in a trial or a shooting field. Another way to perform this exercise is for you to throw out some balls on a Thursday and send your dog to collect them on Sunday, being sure by this time that you will have forgotten where you threw them and that in any case the scent will be poor.

Your dog is now fully trained and you have gained some experience of handling. Your dog may have been run in a novice stake or two and you have noticed his faults under stress and have straightened him out, preferably immediately after the trial is over and in any case the following day. A few further exercises for the trained dog may now be practised. The American dummy-thrower can be used to advantage. Choose a line of trees with a hedge—or a sloping bank leading up to a line of trees—and throw the dummy well out over the trees as if it were a high-flying pheasant. The dog cannot mark the fall nor can you see where your dog is working. Then send him out. If he does not mark in these difficult conditions, wait and see whether he will come back to look for you to give him fresh directions or if he will get worried and lost and hunt wildly. A friend stationed at a vantage point can tell you what the dog is doing, but you must leave the dog alone to work out his own salvation. Or throw an unmarked dummy into the wood. Send the dog in and notice whether he comes back to look for you. Then send him back again each time he appears.

The fully trained dog, however, should only come back once in these circumstances. Having been told for the second time to 'get on', 'get on out', he should realise that he has got to get well out and to go on hunting until he has either found or is recalled by whistle. By this time he should have learnt perseverance and independence; if he hunts close to you and comes back several times to look, a judge will be quite correct in marking him down a little. All the handler can do to help him is to give an occasional click.

It is now time to lay a trail, at first with freshly shot game. A long cord is necessary for this with the game tied to the middle. Your friend holds one end and you the other with fifty yards between you so as not to leave foot scent. Lay a couple of trails with a bird at the end of each. Send your dog to the 'fall' or beginning of the trail and watch him puzzle out the line. Later do it with a bird which has been shot several hours previously and then lay one trail with no bird at the end. Let the dog run along the scent and, after giving him due time to decide that the bird is not there, recall him and send him along the other trail so that he will find a bird at the end of it. Thus you teach him to follow runners, and also watch and learn how he works.

Another exercise is to work in the dusk when you cannot see your dog. Throw a dummy out in these difficult conditions and see if the dog can mark it as it falls against the skyline. When you make a signal, have a handkerchief in your hand to help him, so that he can more easily see the movement of your arm. Dusk is also the time when wild rabbits lie out in the fields and you should exercise your dog amongst them.

Every opportunity must now be taken to give your dog experience in waist-high kale. In these difficult conditions it is permissible for the voice to be used as the dog cannot see you and you cannot see him. Probably, he will, however, jump up to look at you if he hears your whistle or is lost, to see what direction you want him to take. Kale and bolting beet always seem to make the dogs more disobedient. Whether it is the rustle of the kale about his ears, or the many tracks of birds in the kale, I do not know, but I find that these conditions make handling very difficult, and on field trials the handler is always meeting them. It is therefore important in kale to send your dog out right. Clear a space for yourself and the dog and with due accuracy send him on his way. Do not move from this spot or he will lose you, as in all probability he comes back to you by following his own foot scent.

It is very easy to become discouraged during dog training, more easily still when the dog has been taken to a trial and fails to come up to expectation. However, provided the basic material is good and the groundwork of training is carefully taught, there is no reason why the amateur trainer should not hold up his head and win even against professionals and men of wide experience. However, if the amateur tries to hurry his training or skimp the basic exercises, he will suffer for it in the final result.

Having been to a trial and come back early, happy is the trainer who can say to his dog, 'Well, we have made a mess of it but I like you and I wouldn't bring back any other dog but you. Next time, or the time after or the time after that you and I will have the luck and things will go right, and we shall win—and if we don't it won't matter, for I know you know your job, and next time I'll try to help you a little bit more. As a team we shall eventually make it.'

It may be thought that this book has outlined rather a mechanical method of training. This is true, but to train a human being or an animal, the basic principles must of necessity be mechanical to get the best results. However, as every animal is different, the differences must be studied and allowed for. Don't worry about game—the real work must be done on dummies. If your dog and you are working as a team you will find that your dog will look up at you with his brown eyes when a pheasant drops and say, 'May I go out and collect it?' He will not fix his eyes on the pheasant and say, 'I am going to run in unless you prevent me.' I offer this thought: that it is far easier to train a dog than to handle him (until you have gained confidence) when you have trained him. You must know your dog and what he is up against out there.

The professional handler never takes his dog into a trial before he thinks it is ready; thus he preserves his reputation. Some dogs develop early, some are slow developers, so the age of the dog and the time spent on training him are of little importance. Your dog is now fully trained—he will never forget his training. You can now take up fishing, or train another puppy—easy, isn't it? Don't say 'no'—not in front of the dog!

> Let us conclude as we began by quoting from Nicholas Cox:
> Exercise herein preserveth Health, and increaseth Strength and Activity. Others inflame the hot Spirits of young men with roving Ambition, love of War, and seeds of Anger: But the Exercise of Hunting neither remits the Minde to Sloth nor Softness, nor (if it be used with moderation)

hardens it to inhumanity; but rather inclines men to good Acquaintance, and generous Society. It is no small advantage to be endured to bear Hunger, Thirst and Weariness from ones Childhood; to take up a timely habit of quitting ones Bed early, and learning to sit well and safe upon an Horse. What innocent and natural delights are they, when he seeth the Day breaking forth, those Blushes and Roses which Poets and Writers of Romances only paint, but the Huntsman truly courts? When he heareth the chirping of small Birds pearching upon their dewy Boughs? When he drinks in the fragrancy and coolness of the Air? How jolly is his Spirit. When he suffers it to be imported with the noise of Bugle-Horns, and the baying of Hounds, which leap up and play round about him.

Nothing doth more recreate the Minde, strengthen the Limbs, whet the Stomach, and chear up the Spirit, when it is heavy, dull, and overcase with gloomy Cares: from whence it comes, that these delights have merited to be in esteem in all Ages, and even amongst barbarian Nations, by the Lords, Princes, and highest Potentates.

Let us conclude it with a persuasion to all generous Souls not to slight this noble and worthy Exercise, (wherein is contained so much health and pleasure) for the besotting Sensualities, and wicked Debaucheries of a City, in which the course of Nature seems to be inverted, Day turn'd into Night, and Night into Day; where there is little other Recreation but what Women, Wine, and a Bawdy Play can afford them; whereby, for want of Labour and Exercies, Mens Bodies contain as many Diseases as are in a sick Hospital.

APPENDIX 1

Retriever Societies, including Field Trial Societies, and their secretaries

(Some of these societies run training classes and hold working tests)

BIRMINGHAM AND DISTRICT GUNDOG AND TERRIER CLUB Mr. J. Gibson Barbour, 32 Gravelly Hill, Birmingham 23.

BRISTOL AND WEST WORKING GUNDOG SOCIETY Mr. R. A. Davis, Fairlawn, Back of Kingsdown Parade, Cotham, Bristol 6.

BRITISH STEEL CORPORATION (P.T.) F.T. SECTION Mr. J. Carter, Home Farm Cottage, Coldbrook Park, Abergavenny, Gwent.

CAMBRIDGESHIRE FIELD TRIAL SOCIETY Mrs. M. J. Curtis, The Moors, Whittlesford, Cambridge.

CHESHIRE, NORTH WALES AND SHROPSHIRE RETRIEVER AND SPANIEL SOCIETY Mr. K. J. Scandrett, Hill House, Westhope, Hereford, HR4 8BU.

CHILTERN GUNDOG TRAINING CLUB Mr. T. K. Bradbury 2 The Hale, Wendover, Bucks.

CLWYD RETRIEVER CLUB Mrs. J. G. Bailey, Gunstock Kennels, Whitford, Holywell, Clwyd, CH8 9AL.

CORNWALL GUNDOG CLUB Mr. F. W. Harris, 5 Cornwall Terrace, Trehaverne, Truro.

COVENTRY AND DISTRICT GUNDOG SOCIETY Mrs. H. E. Pearson, 126 Rugby Road, Binley, Coventry.

CURLEY RETRIEVER CLUB Mr. J. F. Spooner, 104 Lovely Lane, Warrington, Lancs.

DUKERIES (Notts) GUNDOG CLUB Major A. W. G. Scott, Croft House, Tideswell Lane, Eyam, Sheffield S30 1RD.

EAST ANGLIAN LABRADOR RETRIEVER CLUB Mrs. L. G. Kinsella, The Mount, Fingringhoe, near Colchester, Essex.

EASTERN COUNTIES RETRIEVER SOCIETY Mrs. C. A. Wentworth-Smith, The Old Rectory, Swardeston, Norwich, NOR 95W.

ESSEX FIELD TRIAL SOCIETY Mrs. L. K. Kinsella, The Mount, Fingringhoe, near Colchester, Essex.

FLAT-COATED RETRIEVER SOCIETY Mrs. J. M. Marsden, Brock Cottage, Claughton-on-Brock, Preston PR3 0PP.

APPENDIX I

FORTH AND CLYDE GUNDOG ASSOCIATION Mrs. M. Paton, Loanside Cottage, Clackmannan, Clackmannanshire, Scotland.
GAMEKEEPERS' NATIONAL ASSOCIATION Mr. R. Mundle, 54 Lochfield Road, Dumfries, DG2 9BH.
GOLDEN RETRIEVER CLUB Mrs. J. Lumsden, Little Millbrook, Nutley, Sussex.
GOLDEN RETRIEVER CLUB OF SCOTLAND Mr. J. A. Calvert, Ronette, Kilmalcolm, Renfrewshire.
GOLDEN RETRIEVER CLUB OF WALES Mrs. F. E. Allan, 9 Glasfryn Wafen, Llanelli, Gwynedd.
GOYT VALLEY GUNDOG SOCIETY Mrs. L. Wade, Fourfurn Paddocks, London Road, Adlington, near Macclesfield, Cheshire
HAMPSHIRE GUNDOG SOCIETY Mrs. J. Munday, Sharland, Grayshott, Hindhead, Surrey.
HERTS, BEDS, BUCKS, BERKS AND HANTS RETRIEVER SOCIETY Mrs. F. Wood, Herbert's Cottage, Aston Upthorpe, Didcot, Oxon.
HIGHLAND GUNDOG CLUB Mrs. M. Smith, Norleigh Kennels, Leitchfield, Ardersier, Inverness.
INTERNATIONAL GUNDOG LEAGUE RETRIEVER SOCIETY Mr. J. W. Taylor, 61 Peterborough Road, Castor, near Peterborough.
KENNEL CLUB 1 Clarges Street, Piccadilly, London W1Y 8AB.
LABRADOR CLUB OF SCOTLAND Mr. R. J. Montgomery, Cedar Lodge, Kilsyth, Glasgow, G65 0GA.
LABRADOR RETRIEVER CLUB Lt.-Cdr. P. A. Whitehead, Brookmead, East Grinstead, Salisbury, Wiltshire.
LABRADOR RETRIEVER CLUB OF NORTHERN IRELAND Mr. A. J. Kilpatrick, 16 Corby Drive, Lisburn, Co. Antrim.
LOTHIANS AND BORDERS GUNDOG ASSOCIATION Mr. I. Meiklejohn, 11 Marchmont Street, Edinburgh, EH9 3EY.
MERSEYSIDE GUNDOG CLUB Mrs. J. H. Corrin, Mann Villa, Prescott Road, Melling Mount, Melling, Liverpool.
MIDLAND COUNTIES FIELD TRIAL SOCIETY Mrs. M. Bertrand, Cadge & Colman Ltd., East Station Road, Peterborough
MIDLAND COUNTIES LABRADOR RETRIEVER CLUB Mrs. R. H. B. Hayes, Humby Mill, near Grantham, Lincs.
MIDLAND GUNDOG SOCIETY Mr. G. A. O. Jenkins, Llangunnock, Three Ashes, South Hereford.
MID-WESTERN GUNDOG SOCIETY Mrs. E. J. Walker, Springhill, near Pershore, Worcs.
NORFOLK GUNDOG CLUB Mr. B. G. Colman, 6 Cedar Close, Downham Market, Norfolk.

APPENDIX I

NORTHERN DOG CLUB (MIDDLESBROUGH) Mr. A. E. Rutherford, 47 Stephenson Street, North Ormesby, Middlesbrough.
NORTHERN GOLDEN RETRIEVER ASSOCIATION Mrs. M. Dawson, The Poplars, Donington, Northorpe, Spalding, Lincs.
NORTH OF ENGLAND GUNDOG ASSOCIATION Mr. D. M. Douglas, Frogfield, Laurencekirk, Kincardineshire.
NORTHUMBERLAND AND DURHAM LABRADOR RETRIEVER CLUB Miss E. Smith, 29 High Street, Gosforth, Newcastle-upon-Tyne 3.
NORTH WEST LABRADOR RETRIEVER CLUB Mrs N. Thornton, 6 Skippool Avenue, Poulton-le-Fylde, Lancs.
NORTH WEST COUNTIES FIELD TRIAL ASSOCIATION Mr. M. Walsh, 8 Patterdale Avenue, Fleetwood, Lancs.
RETRIEVER SOCIETY (INTERNATIONAL GUNDOG LEAGUE) Major M. P. E. Evans, Welbarn House, Moulsford, Berks.
SCOTTISH FIELD TRIALS ASSOCIATION Mr. J. Blair, 1 Abbortsford Road, Bearsden, near Glasgow.
SCOTTISH GUNDOG ASSOCIATION Mr. I. Johnston, Welston, Bow Road, Auchermuchty, Fife, KY14 7AG.
SOUTH EASTERN GUNDOG SOCIETY Mrs. P. Hales, White Cottage, North Chailey, Lewes, Sussex.
SOUTH OF ENGLAND GUNDOG CLUB Mr. D. J. Williams, 70 Cannon Hill Lane, Merton Park, London, SW20.
SOUTHERN AND WESTERN COUNTIES FIELD TRIAL SOCIETY Mrs. M. L. Barrenger, Lane End House, Woodlands St. Mary, Newbury, Berks.
SOUTH WESTERN GUNDOG CLUB Mrs. K. G. Holmes, Monkton House, Pinhoe, Exeter.
SOUTH WEST SCOTLAND GUNDOG ASSOCIATION Mrs. G. S. Campbell, Montgreenan Kennels, Kilwinning, Ayrshire.
STRATHMORE WORKING GUNDOG CLUB R. W. Methven, Lauriston, Inchture, Perthshire.
THREE RIDINGS LABRADOR CLUB Mr. C. W. Chase, Holly Bank, Barton on Humber, South Humberside, DN19 7DF.
ULSTER GOLDEN RETRIEVER CLUB Mr. M. A. Kennedy, Goltrieve Kennels, Ballyrickard, Comber, Co. Down.
ULSTER GUNDOG LEAGUE Mr. A. C. M. Rountree, The Old Manse, Drumlegagh, Omagh, Co. Tyrone.
ULSTER RETRIEVER CLUB Mr. H. A. Wilson, Nesfield House, 71 Queensway, Lisburn, Co. Antrim.
UNITED GUNDOG BREEDERS' ASSOCIATION Mr. G. E. Woodcock, 12 Newbridge Gardens, Tettenhall, Wolverhampton.

UNITED RETRIEVER CLUB   Mrs. D. Compton, Fox Close, Stonely, Huntingdon, PE18 0EH.
UTILITY GUNDOG SOCIETY   Mrs. P. Steele, Gosdens Heath, Lodsworth, Petworth, Sussex.
WAVERLEY GUNDOG ASSOCIATION   Mrs. M. R. Barr, 22 Corbiehill Place, Edinburgh 4.
WEST DARTMOOR WORKING GUNDOG CLUB   Mr. I. T. Gussey, Brooking Lodge, Meavy Lane, Yelverton, Devon.
WEST OF ENGLAND LABRADOR RETRIEVER SOCIETY   Mr. L. J. Harding, Coombe Cross, Dittisham, Nr. Dartmouth, Devon.
WELSH KENNEL CLUB   Mrs. M. M. Leopard, Lower Kimbolton Farm, Leominster, Hereford, HR6 0JA.
WEST MIDLAND FIELD TRIAL SOCIETY   Mr. C. Sutcliffe, Netherwood Farm, Bromley Wood, Abbots Bromley, Rugeley, Staffs., WS15 3AG.
YELLOW LABRADOR CLUB   Mr. H. W. Clayton, Ardmargha Cottage, Brightampton, Witney, Oxon, OX5 7QQ.
YORKSHIRE GUNDOG CLUB   Mr. B. G. Spencer, Moor Lodge, Scawby, Brigg, Yorks., DN20 9NG.
YORKSHIRE RETRIEVER FIELD TRIAL SOCIETY   Mr. R. F. Bilton, Rolston Hall, Hornsea, Yorks.

APPENDIX 2

GUIDE TO FIELD TRIAL JUDGES
Issued by the Kennel Club Field Trials Committee

These notes are designed to assist Judges in selecting the best shooting dogs. They are not intended to be rules, as these have already been laid down by the Kennel Club. The Field Trial Rules and Regulations and also the Field Trial Council recommendations, approved by the Kennel Club Field Trials Committee, can be obtained from the Kennel Club free of charge.

No Judge should accept an invitation to judge Trials unless he is fully conversant with these Rules and Regulations and has studied the Guide to Field Trial Judges.

13 September, 1977

RETRIEVERS

1. At the start of a Field Trial, Judges should make sure that they have the correct dogs in the line, lowest number on the right.

2. Judges should take gamefinding to be of the first importance in Field Trials.

3. Judges at Open Retriever Stakes are advised to ask their Guns not to shoot directly over a dog when it is out working. In Puppy, Novice and Non-Winner Stakes, Judges are advised to ask their Guns not to shoot when a dog is out working.

4. All wounded game must be gathered as expeditiously as possible and must be killed at the earliest opportunity. Wounded game must be recovered before dead game. If a Judge cannot gather wounded game, he must be careful to depute this task to the official handler and dog appointed for this purpose.

5. If a bird is shot very close to a dog which would make the retrieve of no value, the Judge should pick the bird by hand or offer it to another Judge. During the first round of the Stake, dogs should have the opportunity on game shot by their own guns.

6. After all the dogs have been tried once, Judges may call up for trial any dog at their discretion.

7. Judges should be most careful to see that each dog gets its

chance in the correct order starting with the lowest number on the right. Should dog No. 1 fail, and dog No. 2 be successful, No. 2 still has the first chance in the next retrieve. It is quite unfair to give a dog two first chances in succession and the other dog two second chances. If the two dogs fail on a bird, the Judge should not call fresh dogs into the line to try for the bird until dogs already in the line have been tried. In the concluding stages of a Trial, Judges may use their own discretion as the situation arises.

8. In the first round of a Stake, if the amount of game permits, a dog should have a minimum of two opportunities to retrieve before the next dog is called up, but the actual number of retrieves is at the discretion of the Judges according to the merit of the work done.

9. When a number of dogs have been tried and have failed on a bird, the Judge should not look for it unless all the Judges agree that no more dogs should be tried. Once Judges have looked for and found a bird, no more dogs should be tried on it.

10. Handlers should be instructed where to try from and given reasonable directions as to where the game fell.

11. Good marking is essential in a Retriever as he should not disturb game unnecessarily. Judges should give full credit to a dog which goes straight to the fall and gets on with the job.

12. At a drive, the placing of the dogs shall be at the discretion of the Judge with the lowest number on the right. The Kennel Club Field Trial Rules state that a dog which whines or barks in the opinion of a Judge shall be discarded from the Stake.

13. A dog must walk steadily to heel.

14. The perfect pick up should be quick with a fast return. The handler should not snatch or drag the game from the dog's mouth. Judges should not penalise a dog too heavily for putting a bird down to get a firmer grip, but this must not, however, be confused with sloppy retrieving. A good gamefinding dog should not rely on the handler to find the bird. He should, however, be obedient and respond to his handler's signals when necessary. Dogs showing gamefinding ability and initiative should be placed above those which have to be handled on to their game. Usually, the best dog seems to require the least handling. He appears to have an instinctive knowledge of direction and makes difficult finds look simple and easy. Steadiness to fur is most important and, where possible, dogs should be given fur to retrieve.

15. If a dog is performing indifferently on a runner, it should be called up promptly. If three or more dogs are tried on a runner, the work of all these dogs must be assessed in relation to the order in which they are tried.

16. If a bird is known to have run, the handlers of the second and subsequent dogs down should be allowed to take their dogs towards the fall, and the first dog also if he has not had a chance to mark the bird.

17. A dog which has its eye wiped on a dead bird should be penalised but all eye-wipes should be treated on their merits. If a dog shows ability by acknowledging the fall and making a workmanlike job of the line, it should not automatically be barred from the Prize List by failing to produce a bird, providing that the bird is not collected by another dog, tried by judges on the same bird.

18. All game should be examined for signs of 'hard mouth'. A hard-mouthed dog seldom gives visible evidence of hardness. He will simply crush in one or both sides of the ribs. Blowing up the feathers will not disclose the damage. Place the bird on the palm of the hand, breast upwards, head forward, and feel the ribs with finger and thumb. They should be round and firm. If they are caved in or flat, this is definite evidence of hard mouth. Be sure the bird reaches your co-judges for examination. There should be no hesitation or sentiment with 'hard mouth'—the dog should be discarded. A certain indication of a good mouth is a dog bringing in a live bird whose head is up and eye bright. Superficial damage, if any, in this case can be ignored. At times, the rump of a strong runner may be gashed and look ugly. Care should be taken here, as it may be the result of a difficult capture or lack of experience in mastering a strong runner by a young dog. Judges should always satisfy themselves that any damage done has been caused by the dog, not by the shot or fall, and in cases of doubt, the benefit should be given to the dog. Handlers should be given the opportunity of inspecting the damaged game in the presence of the Judges, but the decision of the Judges is final.

19. If more than one bird is down and the dog changes birds on his way back, he should be severely penalised.

20. The standard of work in Stakes carrying Field Trial Championship status should be higher than in Novice, Non-Winner and Puppy Stakes, where more leniency is allowed.

21. Judges should keep their opinions strictly to themselves and

act on what happens on the day or days of the Trials at which they are judging, forgetting past performances at previous Trials.

22. Judges are advised to place each dog in a category such as A, B and C, according to the work done at the end of each round.

23. In the concluding stages of a Trial, the dogs should all be in the centre under all the Judges.

24. It is advisable to take short notes of each dog's work and not to trust to memory.

25. It is in the interests of all Field Trial supporters that Judges should be as courteous and co-operative as possible with the Host and Steward of the Beat and fall in with their arrangements. This goes a long way towards making a success of the Trial and the possibility of receiving an invitation for another year.

26. **Summary of points**

Eliminating faults: Hard mouth—Whining or barking—Running in and chasing—Out of control—Failing to enter water.

Major faults: Failing to find game—Unsteadiness at heel—Eye wipe—Disturbing ground—Slack and unbusinesslike work—Noisy handling—Poor control—Changing birds.

Credit points: Natural gamefinding ability—Nose—Marking ability—Drive—Style—Quickness in gathering game—Control—Quietness in handling—Retrieving and delivery.

APPENDIX 3

Extracts from
KENNEL CLUB FIELD TRIAL RULES
10 March 1977
Amended 13 September 1977, 14 December 1977
and 6 June 1978

1. Definitions In these Rules and in any Regulations for the time being in force, unless the contrary intention appears:

(a) Words importing the male sex shall include the female.

(b) Words in the singular shall include the plural, and words in the plural shall include the singular.

(c) The word month shall mean a calendar month.

(d) The Committee means a duly constituted meeting of the Committee of the Kennel Club, and if and so far as any powers of the Committee have been delegated includes the delegated authority.

(e) Delegated Authority means a duly constituted meeting of a Sub-Committee of the Committee of the Kennel Club, or other body to whom powers have been delegated by the Committee.

(f) A Society means any Club, Society or Association promoting a Field Trial and its duly appointed Committee responsible for the executive work of the Society.

(g) A Field Trial is a meeting for the purpose of holding competitions for the work of dogs in the field.

(h) A Stake is a competition held at a Field Trial.

(i) A Nomination is the right to enter at some subsequent date a dog to compete in a stake.

(j) The Draw is the selection by ballot of the order in which dogs in a stake should compete.

(k) A Prize is a money prize or prize of any description won in a stake, other than a Special Prize.

(l) An Award of Honour is not a prize but may be awarded at the discretion of the Judges to the dog officially placed reserve in any Stake.

(m) A Diploma of Merit is not a prize, but may be awarded at the discretion of the Judges at a Championship Meeting.

(n) A Certificate of Merit is not a prize, but may be awarded at the discretion of the Judges an any stake.

(*o*) The Breeder of a dog is the Owner of the dam at the time of whelping, unless a variation of this definition has been effected under the Regulations for Loan or Use of Bitch for Breeding purposes.

(*p*) An Open Stake is a Stake open to all dogs or a named breed, without restriction as to variety, age or residential qualification of the owner, but it may be limited to a prescribed number decided by ballot.

(*q*) An All-Aged Stake is an Open Stake, but restricted by the regulation of the Society promoting the Field Trials.

2. Registrations The following registrations must be made at the Kennel Club prior to the date of closing of applications for nominations or of the closing of entries if no application for nomination is required, and must be made on forms supplied for the purpose and in accordance with the conditions thereon. (All persons making any registration shall be considered as thereby agreeing to be bound by these rules and regulations, including particularly Rules 13 and 14):

(*a*) The name of a dog and the particulars required on the form. When at the date of closing of applications for nominations or of entries a competitor has applied for but has not received the Kennel Club certificate of registration, the dog shall be entered in the name shown as first choice on the registration form and the name should be followed by the letters 'N.A.F.'

(*b*) The last transfer of ownership of a registered dog.

(*c*) Any change of the registered name of a dog.

(*d*) Re-registration in connection with any error in a previous registration.

(*e*) A name assumed for competition or breeding purposes.

(*f*) The affix of an individual partnership.

(*g*) The loan of a bitch for breeding purposes.

The General Committee may decline an application for any registration or cancel any registration already made.

3. Regulations The General Committee shall have power to make, amend, or cancel Registration for the following purposes:

(*a*) For classification of the breeds.

(*b*) For the registration of dogs' names, prefixes, affixes, pedigrees and other registrations under Rule 2.

(c) With regard to entries in the Kennel Club Stud Book.
(d) For conducting Field Trials.

4. Stud Book Entries Any dog which has won a prize or Reserve or been awarded an Award of Honour, Diploma of Merit, or Certificate of Merit at Field Trials held under Kennel Club Field Trial Rules and Regulations, who complies with the Regulations for entry in the Kennel Club Stud Book, is entitled to free entry in the Stud Book.

5. Refusal of Entries A Society may reserve the right to refuse any entries they may think fit to exclude, without assigning any reason for so doing.

6. Nominations A person applying for a nomination renders himself liable for such fee or fees as are mentioned in the Schedule in accordance with the conditions stated therein.

An applicant who is successful in obtaining a nomination may, subject to any restrictions imposed by the Society holding the Trial, substitute a dog before the Trial with another dog owned by him.

7. Prize Money All prize money must be paid within a month of the date of the Field Trial, and paid subject to return in the event of a subsequent disqualification.

8. Objections and Disqualifications An objection to a dog must be made to the Secretary of the Society in writing at any time within twenty-one days of the last day of the meeting upon the objector lodging with the Secretary the sum of £2, which shall be forfeited if the objection prove frivolous. Should any objection be made which cannot at the time be substantiated or disproved, the dog may be allowed to compete under protest, the Secretary retaining any winnings until the objections has been withdrawn or decided upon.

Any appeal to the General Committee must be lodged within fourteen days of the decision being given against which it is desired to appeal.

No spectator, not being the owner of a dog competing, or his accredited representative has the right to lodge any objection to a dog or to any action taken at the meeting unless he be a member of the Committee of the Society, or the General Committee of the Kennel Club or a Steward.

A dog may be disqualified by the General Committee from winning any award, whether an objection has been lodged or not, if proved amongst other things to have been:

(a) Entered at a Field Trial not recognised by the General Committee.
(b) Entered by a person disqualified or suspended under Kennel Club Rules.
(c) Not entered for the Field Trial in accordance with the Regulations of the Kennel Club and the Trial and with the details recorded at the Kennel Club.

If a dog is entered in a Stake for which it is ineligible and is not withdrawn before the commencement of the Stake, the dog will be disqualified.

The owner of a dog disqualified for any of the above reasons is liable to forfeit all nomination and entry fees made for and all prize money won by such a dog.

The General Committee shall have power to inflict fines upoon owners and handlers who have made breaches of Kennel Club Field Trial Rules or Regulations or the Regulations of the Trial, and in the event of such fines or prize money not being paid within the time stipulated by the General Committee, the owner or handler may, at the discretion of the General Committee, be dealt with as if a complaint under Field Trial Rule 13 had been lodged against him, or them, and proved to the satisfaction of the General Committee.

9. The Title of Field Trial Champion The following dogs shall be entitled to be described as Field Trial Champions:

RETRIEVERS

(i) The winner of the Retriever Championship Stake or
(ii) A dog which wins two first prizes at two different Field Trials in Open or All-Aged Stakes for Retrievers.

One of these wins must be in a stake open to all varieties of Retrievers. In order to qualify both stakes must be for not more than 12 nominations with one day allotted for judging and not more than 24 nominations with two days allotted for judging. In 12 dog stakes there must be no fewer than 8 runners and in 24 dog stakes no fewer than 16 runners in order for the stakes to qualify.

Before a Retriever is entitled to be described as a Field Trial Champion it must also have sat quietly at a drive and have passed a water test. These conditions must have been fulfilled at the Championship, in a Field Trial Stake before two Panel A Judges or at a subsequent special test before two Panel A Judges.

10. Championship Stakes The conditions governing Championship Stakes shall be decided by the General Committee and these conditions shall be published as early as possible each year.

11. Order of Merit following Disqualification If a prize winner be disqualified, the dogs next in consecutive order of merit, if so placed by the Judge, and awarded not less than Reserve, shall be moved into the higher places in the Prize List and such placings shall thereupon become the awards.

12. The Kennel Club Disciplinary Sub-Committee The General Committee shall appoint a Sub-Committee (to be known as the Disciplinary Sub-Committee). This Sub-Committee shall have power to co-opt Members of the General Committee to consider particular cases. It shall be the duty of such Disciplinary Sub-Committee to make preliminary investigations into the matter of any complaints or allegations which any person or body may seek to prefer under Rules 13 or 14. In the event of the Secretary of the Kennel Club becoming aware of any matter or matters in respect of which he is of the opinion that consideration should be given with a view to action being taken under Rules 13 or 14, he shall report the same to the Disciplinary Sub-Committee, who shall instruct him whether or not he shall prefer any complaint against any person or persons. No member of the Disciplinary Sub-Committee shall take part in any proceedings which may be brought before the General Committee under Kennel Club Field Trial Rules 13 or 14, and no person who has assisted the Sub-Committee in accordance with the provisions of Rule 9, Part III of the Constitution of the Kennel Club shall take part in any further proceedings that may be taken in any case he has assisted.

13. Disciplinary Powers of the Committee
(i)   The General Committee shall have power to inquire into and deal with any complaint which may be made against any

person who has submitted to the jurisdiction of the Kennel Club.

A complaint may be made in respect of either

(a) Any act or conduct in regard to a dog or any matter connected with, arising out of or relating to a Field Trial, or to these Rules or any Regulations made by the General Committee which in the opinion of the General Committee is discreditable or prejudicial (or calculated to be prejudicial) to the interests of the canine world; or,

(b) Any default or omission in regard to any matter connected with a Field Trial or to these Rules or any Regulations made thereunder.

(ii) PENALTIES.

(a) The General Committee, if any complaint under paragraph (i) (a) of this Rule is proved to their satisfaction, shall have power to inflict any or all of the following penalties:

(1) To suspend the person concerned from taking part in or having any connection with or attending any Show, Field Trial, or Working Trial or from acting as an officer for any canine society.

(2) To disqualify from registration or competition at the discretion of the General Committee, all dogs owned by him or registered in his name, or owned or registered by him jointly with another or others, or owned or registered in the name of a nominee, or the progeny of any dogs owned by him or owned or registered by him jointly with another or others, or owned or registered in the name of a nominee.

(3) To disqualify him from judging at, or taking part in the management of a Show, Field Trial or Working Trial.

(4) To censure and/or warn any such person.

The suspensions and disqualifications under this Rule may be for life or such shorter period as the General Committee shall fix, and the General Committee shall have the power from time to time to remove or modify any suspension or disqualification.

Any persons suspended shall, during the period of such suspension, be not eligible to become or remain a member of any Club or Society registered at or affiliated with the

Kennel Club. If any person suspended under this Rule shall attend any Show, Field Trial or Working Trial, the General Committee shall have power to increase the period of suspension and disqualification.

Any person who shall employ any person suspended or disqualified under this Rule in any capacity in connection with dogs will, if it is proved to the satisfaction of the General Committee that he knew of such suspension or disqualification, be liable to be dealt with as an offender within the meaning of the Rule.

(5) To impose a fine payable at such time and, in the event of non-payment, subject to such penalties as the General Committee may determine.

(b) The General Committee may, if any complaint under paragraph (b) of this Rule is proved to their satisfaction censure and/or warn any person guilty of any such default or omission, or inflict on him a fine, payable at such time as they may determine and if the person makes default in payment he shall so long as such default shall continue, be liable to be dealt with as if he had been suspended under Rule 13 (i) (a).

(c) The General Committee shall have power in any case under this Rule to publish an account of the same, together with the proceedings in respect thereto in the official organ of the Kennel Club, viz. *The Kennel Gazette*, together with the name, description and addresss and, further, to publish the names of such disqualified or suspended persons under this Rule, in two separate 'black lists', which they shall have power to forward to any person or persons concerned, as they may think fit.

(iii) If, on the hearing of any complaint under paragraph (i) (a) of this Rule the General Committee are not satisfied that the complaint is proved but are satisfied that a default or omission under paragraph (i) (b) of this Rule has been proved they may find accordingly and impose the penalties (or any of them) set out in paragraph (ii) (b) of this Rule.

(iv) Any complaint under this Rule may be made by the Secretary of the Kennel Club on the direction of the Disciplinary Sub-Committee, or by the representative of any registered Canine Society on behalf of a Committee of the Society or by an individual who is not suspended or disqualified. Any complaint if made by an individual must be accompanied by a deposit of £5 which may be wholly or partly awarded, if the complaint is dismissed, to the person against whom the complaint is preferred or otherwise dealt with as the General Committee shall think fit. In any case, the complaint shall first be referred to the Disciplinary Sub-Committee who shall give such directions as they think proper to enable the same to be brought before and heard by the General Committee.

(v) When hearing complaints referred to it, the General Committee may appoint a solicitor or barrister to attend the meeting, who need not be a member of the Kennel Club and who may, but need not be, elected as Chairman to preside over the hearing.

(vi) If the General Committee is satisfied that any person has been suspended or disqualified by an overseas Kennel Society with which a Reciprocal Agreement is in force and which has jurisdiction over him they shall suspend or disqualify that person.

(vii) If the General Committee is satisfied that any person has been convicted by a court of cruelty to a dog or of an offence involving dishonesty with regard to a dog, any competition under Kennel Club Rules or a Canine Society, or of an offence which in the opinion of the General Committee is prejudicial to the interest of the canine world, they shall inform the person concerned in a registered letter to his usual or last known place of address of his right to deliver to the General Committee within a period of 21 days a written statement regarding any circumstances of his case which he may wish the General Committee to consider. After considering such written statement or after 21 days have elapsed without such statement being received, the General Committee shall decide on the action, if any, to be taken and shall have power to impose any or all the penalties listed in paragraph (ii) (*a*) of this Rule.

14. Where any person who has not agreed to submit to the jurisdiction of the Kennel Club is alleged to have done any act, or been guilty of any conduct or omission in respect of which a complaint could have been made under Rule 13 if such person had submitted to the jurisdiction of the Kennel Club, such allegation

may be referred to the Disciplinary Sub-Committee who, if satisfied that it would be proper to bring the matter of such allegation before the General Committe, may direct the Secretary of the Kennel Club to invite such person to attend before the General Committee. Any allegation under this Rule may be made in like manner as a complaint under Rule 13 and the Disciplinary Sub-Committee shall give such directions as they think proper to the person or body making such allegation to enable the same to be brought before and heard by the General Committee. The General Committee shall have power to inquire into the matter of any such allegation, and if the same is proved to their satisfaction may impose on the person or body concerned such penalty or penalties as set out in Rule 13 as would be applicable were the act, default or omission the subject-matter of a complaint under Rule 13 save that the Committee shall have no power to impose any fine on any such person.

15. Delegated Powers. The powers conferred on the General Committee under these Rules, except Rule 3 (*a, b* and *c*), are delegated to the Field Trial Committee, but subject to a right of appeal to the General Committee from a decision under Rules 13 and 14.

16. General Committee of Sole Authority The General Committee of the Kennel Club shall be the final court of appeal or umpire in all questions or disputes of any kind whatsoever arising from the competing of any dog at any Field Trials held under the Kennel Club Field Trial Rules, and whether such dispute be between two or more subscribers, or between subscriber or subscribers and the General Committee or Secretary, Veterinary Inspector, or Judge or Judges, of such Field Trials, or between any or more of such parties and another or others of them, and any person or persons acting in any of the capacities above mentioned at any Field Trials held under the Kennel Club Field Trial Rules shall be deemed thereby to agree to refer any disputes which may arise between them or any of them to the General Committee whose decision shall be final and binding.

Extracts from
GENERAL REGULATIONS FOR THE CONDUCT OF FIELD TRIALS

DEFINITIONS

(i) A Puppy is a dog whelped not earlier than the 1st January in the year preceding the date of the Field Trials, but in any stake run in January a dog which was a puppy in the previous month shall be deemed to be a puppy.

1. (a) The Schedule A Society holding a Field Trial must issue a Schedule which is to be treated as a contract between the Society and the public. No modification may be made except by permission of the Kennel Club, followed by advertisement in suitable papers if time permits before the closing of entries. The Secretary of the Society shall send a copy of the Schedule to the Kennel Club within three days of printing. The Schedule must contain:

- (*i*) The date and place of the Field Trial and number of nominations accepted.
- (*ii*) The latest date for applying for a nomination if such is required.
- (*iii*) The latest date for receiving entries.
- (*iv*) The amounts of nomination and/or entry fees and of prize money.
- (*v*) The conditions for the Draw and for intimating acceptance or refusal of nomination.
- (*vi*) A statement that the Field Trial is held under Kennel Club Field Trial Rules and Regulations.
- (*vii*) A definition of any Stake not defined in these Rules or Regulations.
- (*viii*) The names of the Judges, where possible.
- (*ix*) The order in which the Stakes will be run.
- (*x*) A statement of the proportion of entry fee to be returned to entrants should any stake have to be abandoned owing to the weather being unfit.
- (*xi*) For Retrievers and Spaniels, if the Trial includes an Open or All-Aged Stake, an indication of whether that Stake carries a qualification for the Championship.

2. Copy of Rules The Secretary of the Society shall send a copy of these Rules to any applicant and shall have a copy with him or his representative on the ground during a meeting.

3. **Awards** Equal awards for any of the prizes offered at a Field Trial are prohibited.

4. **Record of Entries** The Secretary shall preserve all entry forms for six months after the meeting, and produce any of them to any official body inquiring into an objection or dispute.

5. **Appointment of Judges** The Judges shall be appointed by the Society. The General Committee shall issue to Field Trial Societies Panels of Judges for Field Trials for Retrievers, Spaniels, and Pointers and Setters. Before a Judge can be considered for addition to any panel he must be recommended by a Field Trial Society for which he has judged. The qualifications required before a Judge can be added to a Panel are:

Panel A. Retrievers.

Before a Judge can be added to this Panel he must have judged at least two Open Stakes and two other Stakes run under Kennel Club Field Trial Rules and Regulations and held by two different Societies registered with the Kennel Club.

The compulsory number of Panel A Judges for the various Stakes is as follows:

	Retrievers
Championship	All A
Open and All-Aged Stakes	2 A
Non-Winner and other Stakes	1 A

The General Committee shall have power to add names to the Panels from time to time and also to removes names at their discretion. The General Committee may at its discretion take into account the experience of Judges at Field Trials held under the Irish Kennel Club Field Trial Rules and Regulations when considering the addition of names to the panels.

When there are four Judges for a Stake they must judge in pairs, each pair watching the work jointly of one dog at the same time. Each pair of Judges must decide between themselves which of them is to give the commands.

If only two of the four Judges are on Panel A they must not judge together but must each take one of the Judges not on Panel A as their co-Judge.

No Judge shall shoot at a Field Trial at which he is judging.

The Secretary of a Field Trial must include a copy of the Guide to Field Trial Judges, R(3), issued by the Kennel Club Field Trial Committee, in the Judges' book.

6. Nominations   A nomination is the right to enter at some future date a dog owned and registered at the Kennel Club in the name of the applicant for the nomination. If a partnership of two or more persons make application for a nomination for the partnership, then only one of the partners shall be permitted to apply for a separate nomination for a dog registered at the Kennel Club in his sole ownership. If applications exceed the number of nominations available, the right to a nomination shall be decided by ballot. If a nomination be not returned to the Secretary of the Society by a date specified in the Schedule the applicant will be held to have accepted it and be liable for the full entry fee, unless the Secretary can transfer the nomination to some other applicant.

7. Reducing Prize Money   If the full number of nominations be not applied for or nominations not accepted cannot be transferred to other applicants, the prizes may be reduced at the option of the Society.

The amount of Prize Money offered by a Society may be made to depend on the number of entries received.

8. Order of Running   The Draw shall take place at such time and in such conditions as are stated in the Schedule, and at it each dog must be given the number that accords with its place in the draw, and every dog must be tried in order of draw.

9. Management at Field Trials   The management of a Field Trial shall be entrusted to the Society, who shall decide any disputed question by a majority of those present.

Secretaries of Field Trials must ensure that a handler and dog are always available to pick up wounded game when required.

In no circumstances shall handled dead game be used at a Field Trial except for the purposes of a water test or for a Qualifying Certificate.

10. Weather Conditions   If the Society considers the weather unfit for holding the Trial, the stake or stakes may be cancelled and a proportion of the entry fees, decided by the Society and published in the Schedule, shall be returned to entrants; or a fresh draw may be made and a fresh date fixed for the abandoned stake or stakes.

11. Handling of Dogs If a deputy handles a dog, the owner may be in the line but must take no part in the working of the dog. All handlers must obey the orders of the judges. Handlers will not be allowed to carry in their hand, gun, stick, whip, shooting stick, or lead, whilst handling their dogs, but in cases of physical disability a shooting stick may be carried with the permission of the Judges.

No handler may handle more than three dogs in any single dog Stake for Retrievers.

When there are four Judges at a Retriever Trial there is no objection to relatives of Judges running dogs.

When called up by the Judges, a handler may wear only the armband relevant to the dog being judged.

12. Dogs under Trial The control of all matters connected with dogs under trial shall rest with the Judges of the meeting, but they may call the Secretary to their assistance if they think fit.

The Judges are empowered to turn out of the Stake any dog whose handler does not obey them, or wilfully interferes with another competitor or his dog.

13. Physical Condition Should the members of the Committee present, after consultation with the Judges, consider a dog is unfit to compete by reason of sexual causes or of any contagious disease or from an attack of hysteria occurring on the ground or any other cause which interferes with the safety or chance of winning of his opponents, such dog must be removed immediately from the ground and from the Trials. Any such case is liable to be reported to the Kennel Club and dealt with under Rules 13 or 14.

If a dog competes which has been exposed to the risk of any contagious or infectious disease during the period of six weeks prior to the Field Trial and/or if any dog shall be proved to be suffering at a Field Trial from any contagious or infectious disease, including contagious results of inoculations against distemper, the owner thereof shall be liable to be dealt with under Rule 13.

14. Unpunctuality A dog which is not present when required by a Judge may be disqualified.

15. Discarding Dogs No dog shall be discarded until it has been tried by two Judges except that it shall be discarded if it has run in or chased or if two Judges concur that the dog is out of control of his handler or is held to have a hard mouth, but all the Judges must have examined the injured game before the dog is discarded for hard mouth.

The handler should be given the opportunity of examining the damaged game in the presence of the Judges, but the decision of the Judges is final.

A dog which whines or barks in the opinion of a Judge shall be discarded from the Stake.

In the Retriever Championship Stake the discarding of dogs shall be entirely at the discretion of the Judges.

16. Water Test A Water Test requires a dog to enter water readily and swim to the satisfaction of the Judges. In Retriever and Spaniel Stakes and Stakes for breeds which hunt, point and retrieve, a dog which fails a Water Test shall not receive an award in that Stake. If a Water Test is held, all dogs placed in the awards must have passed this test. A handler is not entitled to ask for a shot to be fired

A Special Water Test conducted in accordance with the provisions of Field Trial Rule 9 – Title of Field Trial Champion must be held between 1 October and 1 February.

17. Awards of Honour, Diplomas of Merit and Certificates of Merit Judges shall be empowered to award Diplomas of Merit in Championship Stakes and Certificates of Merit in all other Stakes to those dogs, apart from the prize winners, which have, in their opinion, acquitted themselves sufficiently well to warrant them.

A dog officially placed Reserve shall receive an Award of Honour or a Certificate of Merit at the discretion of the Judges. At a Championship meeting a dog officially placed Reserve shall receive an Award of Honour or a Diploma of Merit at the discretion of the Judges.

18. Witholding Prizes The Judges are empowered and instructed to withold any prize or award if, in their opinion, the dogs competing do not show sufficient merit.

19. Withdrawal of Dogs No dog entered for competition and once under a Judge at the Trial may be withdrawn from competition without the consent of the Society.

No competitor may leave the field without the permission of the Judges or Society and any dog so removed is liable to disqualification.

20. Impugning Decisions Anyone taking part in a Trial openly impugning the decision of the Judge or Judges shall render himself liable to be reported to the Field Trials Committee of the Kennel Club under the provisions of Kennel Club Field Trial Rule No. 13.

21. Qualifying Certificates A Gundog which has won one or more Challenge Certificates at Shows may be entered for a Qualifying Certificate at a Field Trial Meeting for its breed provided that:
1. For Retrievers, the Society holding the Meeting is recognised for the Retriever Championship and that two of the Judges awarding the Qualifying Certificate appear on the Official Judges Panel A for Retrievers.
   - (*a*) The permission of the Society holding the Trial must be obtained and the dog must be entered on the entry form of the meeting. The fee charged by the Society must not exceed £5.00.
   - (*b*) A dog may not run for a Qualifying Certificate more than three times in all and not more than twice in any one Field Trial season.
   - (*c*) All dogs entered for Qualifying Certificates must be tested during the morning.
   - (*d*) The granting of Qualifying Certificates shall be at the discretion of the Judges at the meeting and all Judges must sign the Certificate.
   - (*e*) Before signing a Certificate the Judges must be satisfied that the dog fulfils the following requirements:
     (1) that the dog has been tested in the line; (2) that the dog

has shown that he is not gun-shy and was off the lead during gunfire; (3) for a retriever, that it hunts and retrieves tenderly; (4) steadiness is not absolutely essential for a Qualifying Certificate.

A Gundog which has won one or more first prizes in a Class for its breed at a Show where Challenge Certificates are offered for the breed, may be entered for a Qualifying Certificate at a Specialist Club Qualifying Trial provided that Judge or Judges of the Trial are on Panel A for the breed and subject to Regulations (*d*) and (*e*) above.

22. Contingencies Any event not provided for in these Rules and Regulations shall be decided by the members present of the Committee of the Society assisted by the Judges, and their decision shall be final.

FIELD TRIAL REGULATIONS FOR RETRIEVERS

1. Competing The dog with the lowest number under each Judge shall be placed on his right. After all the competing dogs have been tried under two judges, the judges may call up at their own discretion any dogs they require further and try them again.

2. Retrieving Fur and Feather All dogs running in Stakes other than Puppy, will be expected to retrieve fur as well as feather. In a Puppy Stake they will not be compelled to retrieve fur.

3. 'Driving' and 'Walking-up' Where possible, all dogs should be tested, driving, walking-up, and in water.

4. Dogs must not wear any form of collar when under the orders of the judges.

INDEX

Age, for buying, 39
   for training, 45
Aims of training, 14, 15 50
Amateur trainers, 12, 124, 158
American standards, 14, 15, 24
Aphorisms, 90 *et seq.*
Area, hunting the, 52, 81–3, 108, 111, 112, 114, 124, 137–8, 147, 155

Bag, in Field Trials, 153
Balls, rubber, 53, 65, 78, 83, 115, 117, 155
Beaters, 132, 154
Blood scent, 118, 138, 156–7
Blood sports, 13
Brailing, 52
Breeding (*see* Inbreeding, Outbreeding, Line-breeding)
Bribery, 59

Car training, 44, 50
Certificate of merit, 136, 141, 168
Check cords, 65
'Come to Daddy', 45, 48, 50, 66, 72, 83
Commands, 66
Control, distant, 85, 86, 116, 117
Costs, 39, 41
Cover, training in, 102, 106, 107, 113, 156, 157
Covert shoots, 127, 151, 153
Cox, Nicholas, 8, 13, 33, 37, 40–1, 92, 158–9
Credit points, 136, 167
Crowd shy, prevention of, 41

Delivery, 48, 50, 60, 61, 72
Diet, 40–1
Discipline, 14, 57–8, 81, 131, 132
Disobedience, 20, 58–61, 115, 122
Down the line, 84, 85
Drives, 134
Dummies, 19, 45, 48, 51, 53, 54, 65, 72, 75, 76, 78, 79, 81, 84, 85, 86, 87, 90, 99, 116, 117, 157
Dummy thrower, 78, 156

Encouragement, to hunt faster, 59, 66
Errors, 121 *et seq.*
Equipment, 65
Excitement, 11, 81, 125, 126
Eyesight (*see* Vision)
Eye wipes, 136, 140, 150

Fall, 17, 19, 77, 116
Faults, 16, 39, 57 *et seq.*, 136, 167
Fear, 20, 32, 44, 99
Feeding (*see* diet)
Fees (*see* costs)
'Find the lady', 85, 86, 115, 116
Field trials, 15, 145 *et seq.*
Fight, distance, 20
Flight, distance, 20
Free running, 14, 15, 81

Game, introduction to, 79, 118, 128–31, 158
Game fair, 137
Gentleman's Recreation, The, 8, 13, 33, 37, 40–1, 92, 158–9

185

186 INDEX

Ground, for training, 45, 46, 50, 51 *et seq.*, 115, 119
Grouse shooting, 130
Guide to field trials and judging, 135, App. 2 and 3
Gun training, 78–9
Guns, 125, 130, 131, 132, 142, 150, 152, 153

Handling, 46 *et seq.*, 65 *et seq.*, 105 *et seq.*
Hard mouth, 11, 61, 126, 130, 136
Hares, 54, 56, 128, 129, 134
Hearing, 19, 116
Heeling, 47–8, 52, 120, 149
History of Labradors, 23–4
Host, in field trials, 152–4
House training, 41–4, 46
Hunting, 48, 50, 71, 81–3, 115–16
Hupping, 46, 66, 69, 83

Inbreeding, 36
Intelligence, 13, 14, 93

Judges' shorthand, 140
Judging, 77, 135 *et seq.*, 147, 149–51
Jumping, fences, 95
  wire, 95
  wall, 101–2
Jumping up, 48

Keepers, 130, 131, 154
Kennels, 42, 45, 76
Kennel Club, 24, 135
Kennel yard training, 46

Leads, 47, 65, 127, 132, 134
Live game, use of, 54, 118

Line-breeding, 36

Marked retrieves, 60, 77, 106, 109–10, 128, 145
Markers, use of, 117
Marking, 76–8, 136
Memory, 22–3, 76–7
Mistakes, of dog, 59 *et seq.*
  of handler, 121 *et seq.*

Non-winner stakes, 135, 164 *et seq.*
Novice stakes, 135, 146, 155, 164 *et seq.*

Obedience, 14, 15, 50, 63, 84, 105, 106
Olfactory fatigue, 31
Open stakes, 135, 137, 146, 164 *et seq.*, 169 *et seq.*
Otter tail, 24
Outbreeding, 36
Out of control, 136

Pack animal, 12, 13, 21
Pens, 54 *et seq.*
Picking up, 130
Pigeons, shooting, 131
  use of, 118
'Pilling', 38
Praise, 44, 50
Prices, 39, 41
Pricked bird, 138
Professional trainers, 11, 12, 16, 125, 143, 144
Progress, 50, 53, 63, 64, 105
Punishment, 13, 18, 44–5, 57–8, 63, 64, 115, 127
Puppy stakes, 164 *et seq.*, 175 *et seq.*

Quarrelling, 13, 127
Quality, 25

Retina, of eye, 17
Retrieving, force method, 61–2
  general, 48, 54, 60–2, 72–3,
    105 et seq., 115–7, 127–32,
    133, 149–51, 155, 157
Retrievers, varieties of, 15
Runners, 126, 130, 150
Running in, 62, 128, 136, 151

Scent, 18–19, 27 et seq., 93
Send-off, 67–8, 76, 87, 116
Shoots, formal, 127 et seq.
  rough, 119–20, 130
Show dogs, 25
Signals, 66 et seq.
Sit (see Hup)
Slow developer, 63, 158
Snipe, introduction to, 129
Stakes, Open (see open stakes)
  Novice (see novice stakes)
Standards, 24–6
Steadiness, 54, 55, 62, 92, 125–6
Stewards, 143
Stop whistle, 66, 69, 74, 83, 84, 93
Suitability, for training, 11, 14, 24, 37–9
Survival of fittest, 35
Swimming (see water work)

Teeth, 24, 25
Temperament, 11, 15–16, 20, 22, 25
Times, for training, 75, 76
Tracks, 77, 84, 94, 157
Training collars, 65
  general, 11–15, 17, 19, 21–2, 38, 39, 44, 50, 75, 76
Trials (see field trials)
Type, 24–5

Unseen retrieves, 76, 89, 111, 112, 115–17, 145, 149–50, 155–6

Vibration sense, 19
Vision, 17–18
Voice, 50, 66–7, 73–4, 113

Walking in line, 152
Walking to heel (see heeling)
Water work, 51, 61, 94–101
Whistles, silent, 65, 66, 69, 74, 83, 84
  horn, 65, 66, 83
Wind, use of, 18–19, 53, 81, 84, 88, 89, 107, 108, 110, 111, 116
Woodcock, introduction to, 79
Working tests, 136, 145–6
Wounded birds, etc. (see runners and pricked birds)

Yipping, 11, 63, 67